T0343487

Cambridge Little Steps 2

Activity Book
Gabriela Zapiain

CAMBRIDGE
UNIVERSITY PRESS

Cambridge Little Steps 2

1 What do you like about school? — 3

2 How do we take care of ourselves? — 17

3 What do we do at home? — 31

4 What can we see on a farm? — 45

5 What do we eat at different times of the day? — 59

6 What different kinds of clothes do we wear? — 73

7 What can we do with our senses? — 87

8 How do we get from one place to another? — 101

9 What do plants need to grow? — 115

Picture Dictionary — 129

1 What do you like about school?

🗨 Say. ✏ Color. ◯ Trace.

cut

paint

glue

color

draw

Key Language: *cut, color, paint, draw, glue.* Children point to and name each action: *paint, draw, color, cut, glue.* Then they color the child and the activity they like the most. Optional: Children trace the initial letters of each word.

3

■ Say. ○ Circle. ✎ Color.

My Favorite Thing

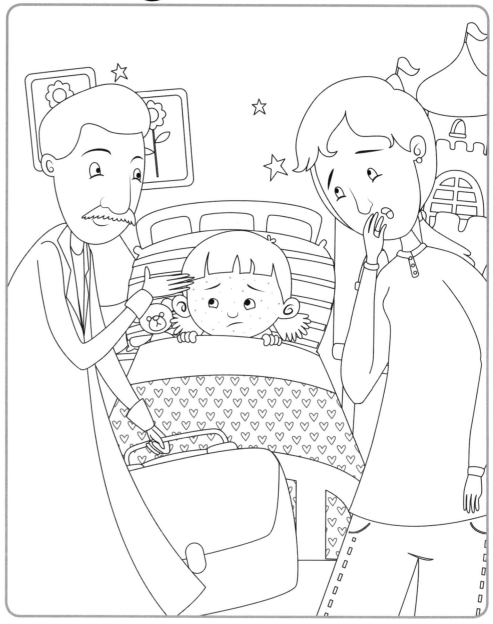

Key Language: *What's the story about? What can you see? house, mouse, teacher, sad, happy.* Children look at the story scenes. Ask the literacy questions. Elicit answers using *I can see ...* Then ask: *Can you see a house / a mouse? Can you see a teacher? Can you see someone sad / happy?* Children circle and then color the items in the pictures.

🗨 Say. ⭕ Circle. ✏ Color.

Key Language: *What's the story about? What can you see? book, sad, happy.* Children look at the story scenes. Ask the literacy questions. Elicit answers using *I can see ...* Then ask: *Can you see someone cutting / coloring? Can you see a book? Can you see someone sad / happy?* Children circle and then color the items in the pictures. Finally, children retell the story in their own words. Provide language as needed.

 Point. ▨ Say. ✎ Color.

Do you like the story?

Key Language: *What is the story about? Think about the story. Can you remember?* Ask the literacy questions, and specifically: *Can you remember the presents Betty received?* Ask: *Which are Betty's presents?* Children point to, name, and color Betty's presents *(coloring book and crayons)*. Finally, ask: *Do you like the story? (Yes. / No.)* Children color the happy face or the sad face.

 Look. 💬 Say. ✏ Color.

Key Language: *clean up, Let's clean up our classroom.* Children look at the scene. Ask: *What are the children doing?* (*cleaning up the paint and paintbrushes, cleaning up the classroom*). Discuss why it is important to keep our classroom clean and tidy. (*So we know where to find toys and books and crayons. So it is a pleasant environment for everyone*). Discuss what we can do to keep our classroom clean. (*Pick up toys or crayons, pencils, etc. Put things back where we found them. Throw garbage away.*) Finally, children color the children who are keeping the classroom clean.

Say. Color. Trace.

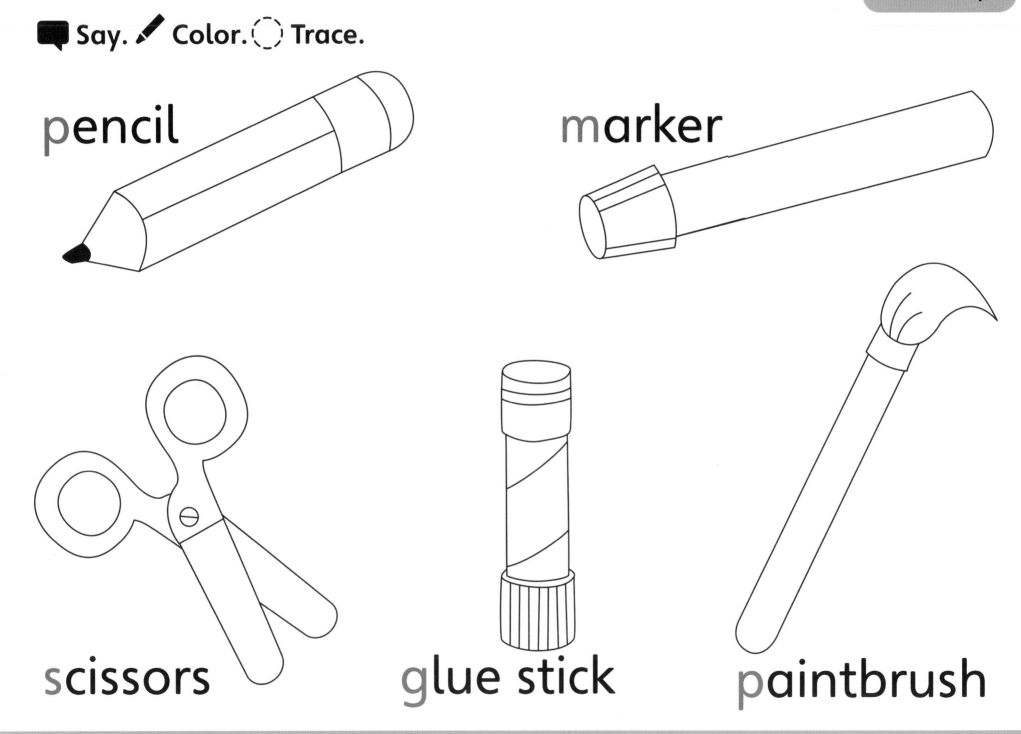

pencil

marker

scissors

glue stick

paintbrush

Key Language: *pencil, marker, paintbrush, glue stick, scissors.* Children point to and name each object: *pencil, marker, paintbrush, glue stick, scissors.* Then they color the items. Optional: Children trace the initial letters of each word.

✋ Count. 💬 Say. ✏ Color.

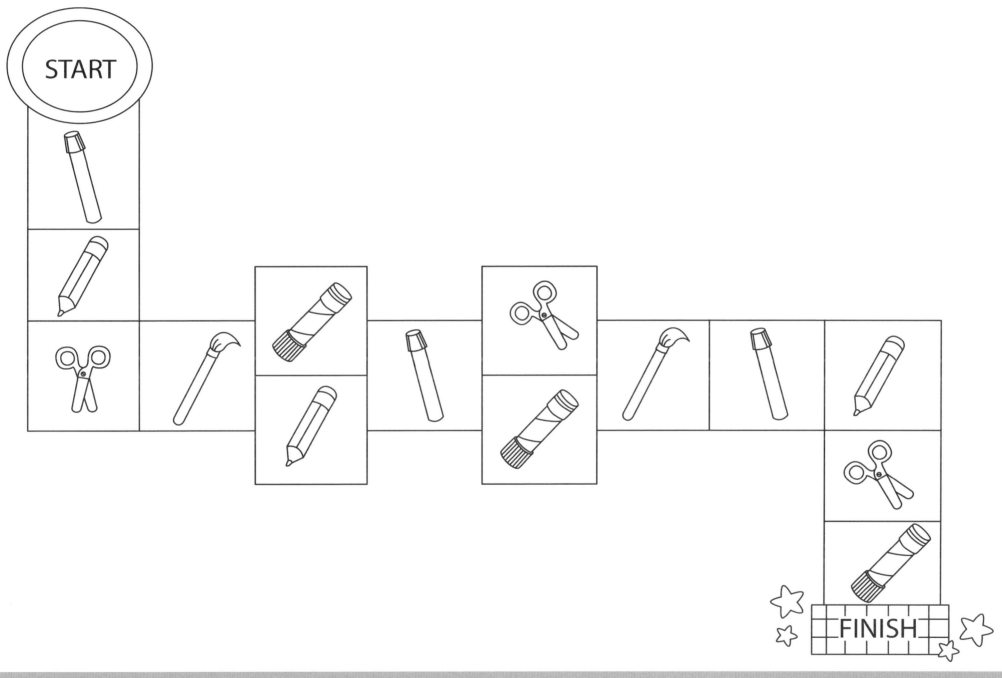

Key Language: *I (draw / paint / stick / cut) with (a pencil / a marker / a paint brush / a glue stick / scissors).* Look at the game together. Identify the start and finish places and then demonstrate how to roll a dice, count and move the corresponding number of squares. Explain that, when children land on a square, they must name the object, say what they do with the object and then color it. Model a few times, saying e.g., *I draw with a pencil. I cut with scissors.* Distribute crayons and dice, then guide and support children as they play in groups.

9

✏️ Color. 💬 Say.

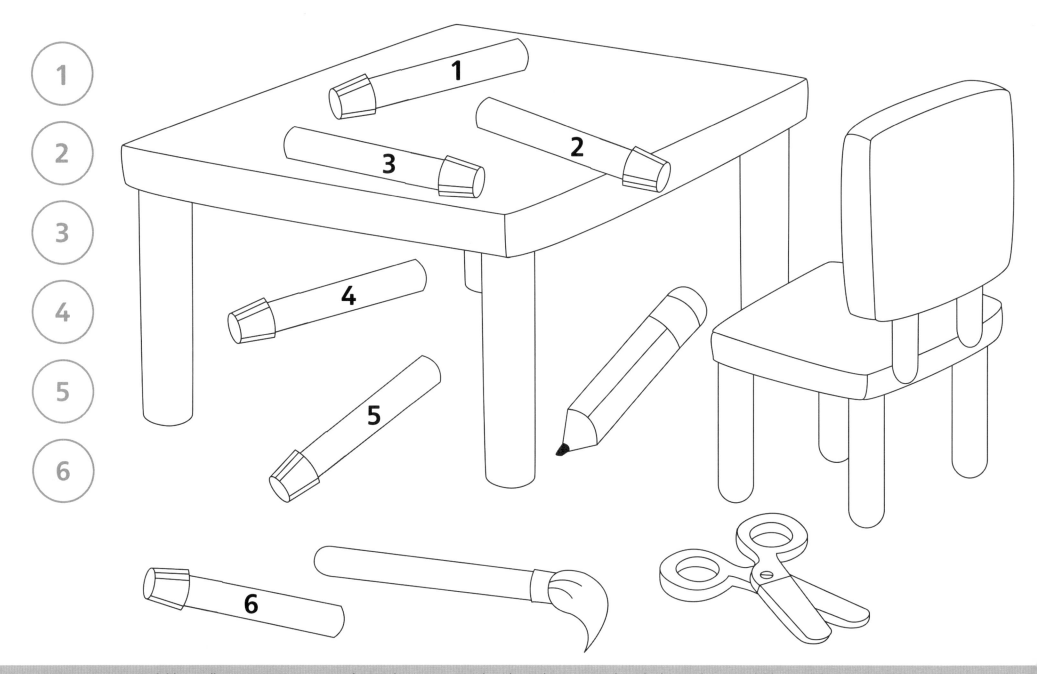

Key Language: *red, blue, yellow, green, orange, purple.* Distribute crayons in the 6 key colors. Point to the color key and instruct children to color, saying: *Color number 1 red.* etc. (2 yellow, 3 green, 4 orange, 5 blue, 6 purple). When they're finished, say a number. Children respond with the correct color. Draw children's attention to the numbers on the markers in the picture. Explain that they should use the color code to color the markers.

 Say. Color. Trace.

listen to stories

sing songs

clean up

eat lunch

play with friends

Key Language: *What do you do at school? listen to stories, sing songs, clean up, eat lunch, play with friends.* Point to each activity and encourage children to repeat as you name each of them. Ask: *What do you do at school?* Children respond by pointing or saying, e.g., *I sing songs (at school).* Children color the activities they do at school. Optional: Children trace the initial letters of each word.

11

💬 Say. ✏️ Draw. ✏️ Color.

Key Language: *What do you like to do? I like to (sing / clean up / play with friends / listen to stories).* Ask: *What do you like to do at school?* Allow several children to answer by pointing to the pictures or by saying, e.g., *I like to sing songs. I like to color with markers. I like to play with friends.* Children draw and color the child in the center of the page to look like themselves. Then they draw lines from this to the activities they like to do. Finally, they present their work and say: *I like to ....*

🗨 Say. ➡➡ Follow. ✏ Color.

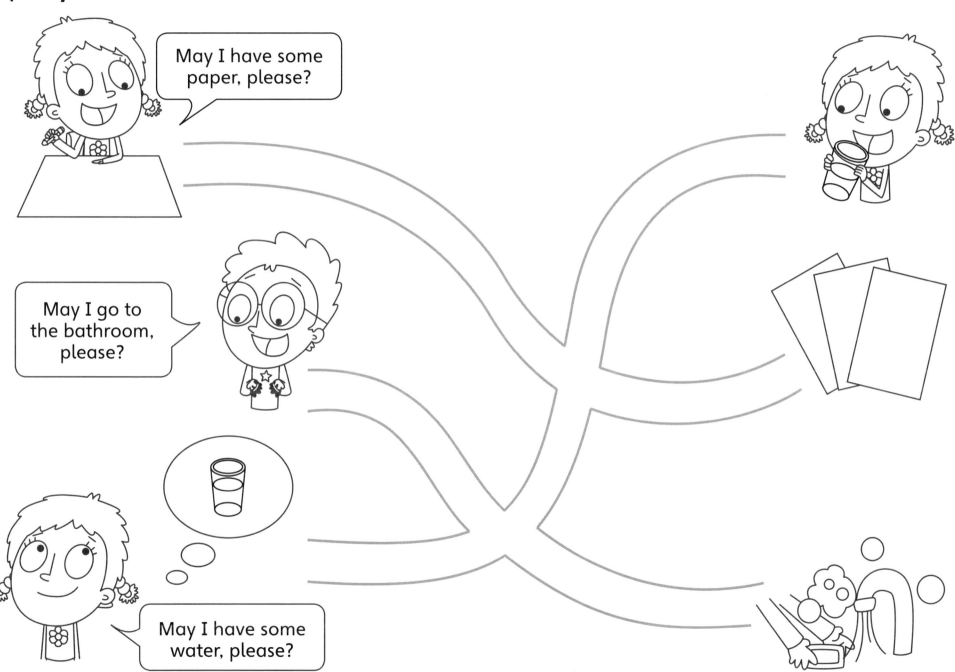

May I have some paper, please?

May I go to the bathroom, please?

May I have some water, please?

Key Language: *May I ..., please? Yes, you may.* Children point to each picture and ask the corresponding question. Allow several children to ask the question, and respond each time with: *Yes, you may.* Then they follow the maze to link each character with what he or she needs. Finally, children color the pictures.

13

👁 Look. 💬 Say. 🖌 Paint.

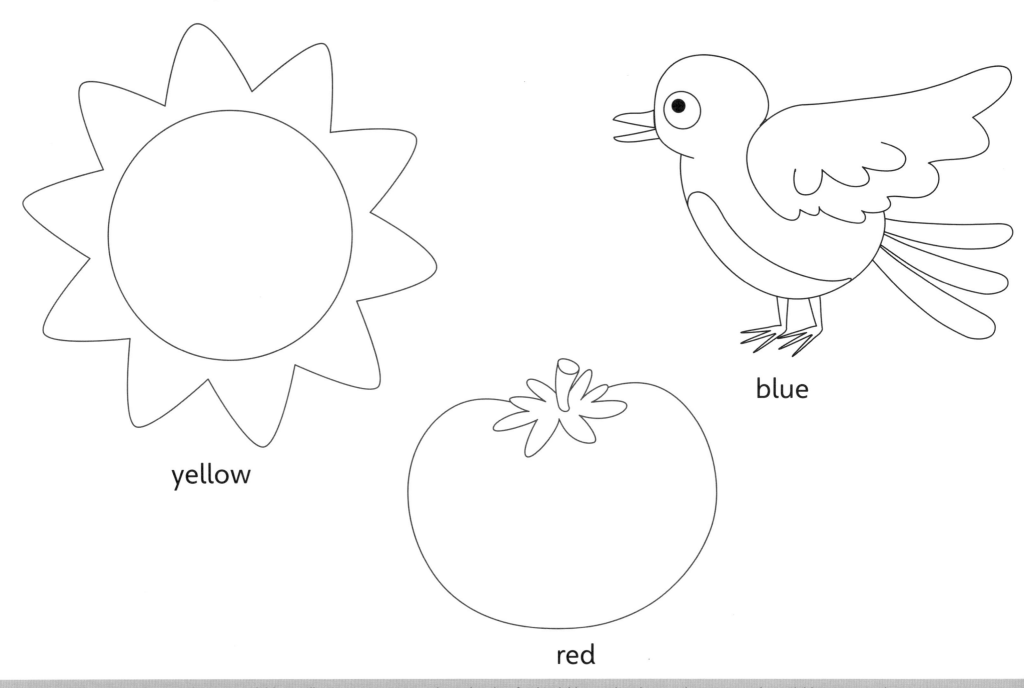

yellow

blue

red

Key Language: *primary colors, It's (red, blue, yellow).* Arrange paint and paintbrushes for the children. Ask: *What are the primary colors?* Children answer, then point to the corresponding paint colors on the desk *(red, blue, yellow).* Children look at the pictures. Ask: *What color is the sun? (Yellow!)* Children paint the sun yellow. Repeat with the remaining pictures. When they're finished painting, children can present their pages, pointing and saying: *It's red. It's blue. It's yellow.*

 Count. Color. Trace.

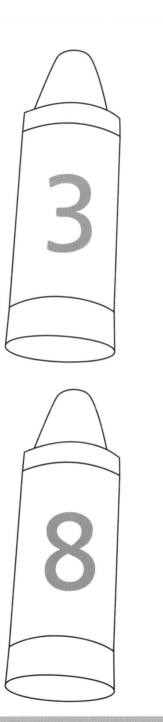
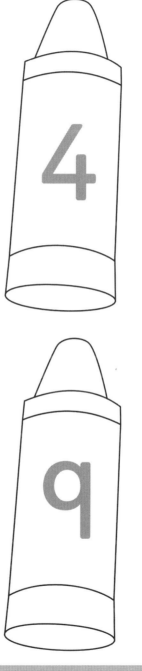
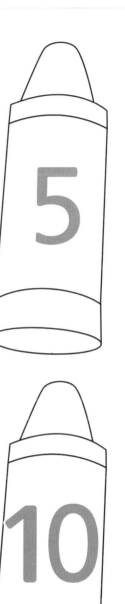

1   2   3   4   5

6   7   8   9   10

Key Language: *How many (crayons) can you see? Let's count: one, two, three, four, five, six, seven, eight, nine, ten.* Ask: *How many crayons can you see? Let's count!* Children count the crayons. Then children point and say the numbers on each crayon. Finally, they color each crayon a different color. Optional: Children trace the numbers.

 **Draw.** **Say.**

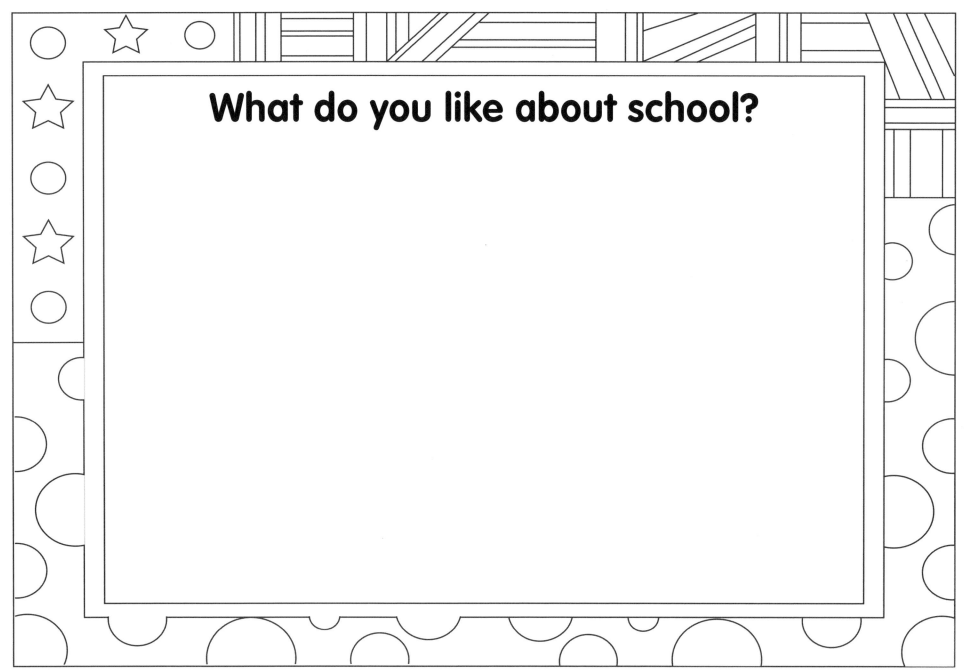

What do you like about school?

Key Language: *paint, draw, color, cut, glue, pencil, marker, paintbrush, glue stick, scissors, I (cut) with (scissors). I like to (listen to stories, sing songs, clean up, eat lunch, play with friends).* Ask the Big Question: *What do you like about school?* Children look back through the unit to recall what they have learned. Then they draw something they've learned inside the frame, such as themselves and friends singing, crayons and markers in different colors, or a clean classroom. Ask volunteers to share their drawings with the class and name what they drew. Finally, answer the Big Question together, using the children's drawings to help.

② How do we take care of ourselves?

💬 Say. ✏️ Color. ⭕ Trace.

wash my face

brush my hair

eat healthy food

put on a jacket

drink water

Key Language: *wash my face, brush my hair, eat healthy food, put on a jacket, drink water.* Ask children the Big Question, and then mime the 5 activities for them to name. Repeat the mimes, and encourage children to copy. Point to each picture and have children say the words. Then instruct children to color the following elements in each picture: *face, hair, food, jacket, water.* Optional: Children trace the initial letters in each vocabulary item while saying the words.

■ Say. ◯ Circle. ✎ Color.

Good Job, Oliver!

Key Language: *What can you see? What's the story about? Who is this character? What is he doing?*, *face.* Children look at the story scenes. Ask the literacy questions. Then ask: *Can you see a face? Can you see a boy washing his face / brushing his hair?* Children circle, then color the child washing his face.

🔊 Say. ⭘ Circle. ✏ Color.

Key Language: *What's the story about? Who / What can you see? What is the character doing?, jacket, lunchbox.* Children look at the story scenes. Ask the literacy questions. Then ask: *Can you see a jacket? Can you see a boy putting on his jacket? Can you see a lunchbox? Can you see Oliver's food? Is it healthy food?* Children circle, then color the items in the pictures. Finally, children retell the story in their own words. Provide language as needed.

◌ Trace. ◼ Say. ✏ Color.

Do you like the story?

Key Language: *What does (Oliver) do in the story? Does this happen in the story?* Look at the first picture together and describe what's happening. Then ask: *What does Oliver do in the story? How does Oliver take care of himself?* Point to each picture and ask, e.g., *Does this happen in the story? Does he wash his face?* Continue with the other pictures, encouraging children to think back to the story and answer *Yes* or *No*. Then they trace the line to show the correct sequence of actions. Retell the sequence from the story together. Repeat with the second sequence. Finally, ask: *Do you like the story? (Yes. / No.)* Children color the happy face or the sad face.

👁 Look. 💬 Say. ✏ Color.

Key Language: *How can we take care of ourselves? We can (wash / eat healthy food / drink water).* Children look at the scene. Ask: *What are they doing?*
(drinking water, riding bikes). Ask: *Are they taking care of themselves? (Yes!)* Discuss why it is important to take care of ourselves. *(So we are healthy and happy.)*
Discuss what else we can do to take care of ourselves. *(Wash, eat healthy food, etc.)* Finally, children color the people who are taking care of themselves.

21

 Say. Match. Trace.

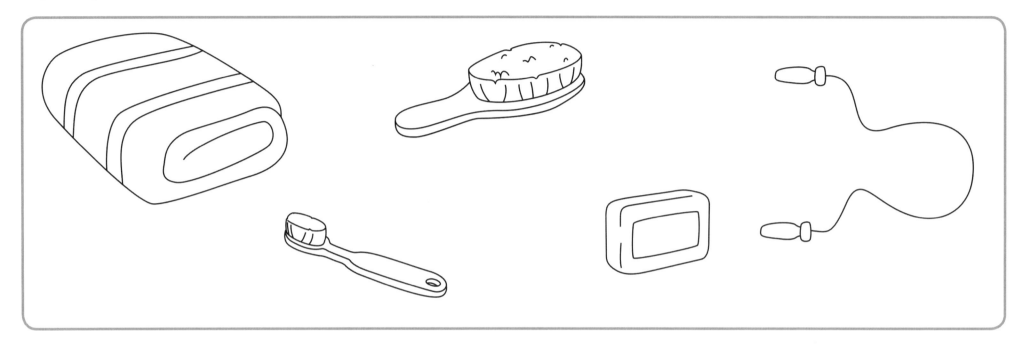

soap

brush

toothbrush

towel

jump rope

Key Language: *soap, brush, toothbrush, towel, jump rope.* Point to the first picture *(towel),* say the word and have children repeat after you. Then ask: *Can you see another towel?* Children find the picture of the towel in the group below and then draw a line to match the two pictures. Continue with the remaining vocabulary items. Optional: Children trace the initial letters of each word.

➜➜ Follow. 💬 Say. ✏️ Color.

Key Language: *He takes care of himself. He washes his hands with soap, brushes his hair / teeth, jumps rope, dries his hands with a towel.* Children follow the path with their finger. For each picture children encounter along the path, they say a sentence about how the boy takes care of himself, e.g., *The boy washes his hands with soap.* Finally, children color the pictures.

23

■ Say. ◯ Trace. ✏ Color.

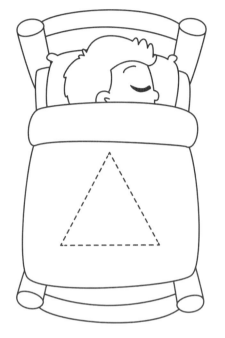

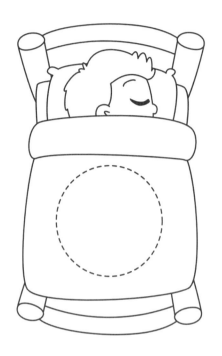

Key Language: *What shape is it? It's a star, circle, square, rectangle, triangle.* Ask children to look at the different beds, point to each blanket and ask: *What shape is this?* Children name the shapes. Then they trace the shapes while repeating the names (e.g., *triangle, triangle, triangle*). Finally, they color the shapes. Children can present their pages, saying: *It's a circle. It's purple.*

 **Say.** ✎ **Color.** ◯ **Trace.**

thirsty

tired

happy

dirty

hungry

sick

Key Language: *tired, thirsty, dirty, hungry, sick.* Point to the first picture and say: *I'm thirsty.* Then point to the next picture and call on a volunteer to say: *I'm tired.* Exaggerate the words and mimic the actions to help children guess the meaning. Continue in this manner until all children have participated. Then children color in the face that shows how they are feeling. Optional: Children trace the initial letters of each word.

25

🗨 Say. ◯ Circle. ✏ Color.

Key Language: *What can s/he do to take care of herself/himself? S/he can (eat healthy food / sleep / drink water / wash / take medicine).* Point to the first picture and say: *She's tired. What can she do to take care of herself?* Direct children's attention to the two choices and ask: *Drink water? Sleep?* Children say the correct answer *(sleep)* and then circle it. Continue with the remaining situations, asking the question, eliciting and repeating the answer, and then allowing children time to circle. Finally, children can color the children and the correct choices: *sick / take medicine, dirty / wash, thirsty / drink water, hungry / eat.*

🔊 Say. 📖 Match. ✏️ Color.

Key Language: *What's the matter? S/he's (hungry / thirsty). S/he needs to (eat / drink)! How does s/he feel? Happy / sad.* Point to the first picture of Leo and ask: *What's the matter? (Leo's / He's hungry.)* Encourage children to rub their tummies mimicking hungry as they say it. Then ask: *What does he need? (He needs to eat.)* Point to the picture showing Leo eating an apple and say: *Leo needs to eat!* Children draw a line to match both pictures. Guide children to the idea that he's eating healthy food, which makes him feel good. Repeat with Mia and thirsty in the same way. Finally, children color the pictures of the happy children, no longer hungry or thirsty.

👁 Look. ⭕ Circle. ✏ Color.

Key Language: *grapes, French fries, lettuce, carrots, tomato, pizza, Is this healthy / unhealthy?* Ask children to look at all the food and say: *Can you see any healthy food? Circle the healthy food.* Identify the healthy food items together (carrot, orange, grapes, pear, apple) as children draw circles around each. Finally children color the healthy food. Discuss *healthy* vs *unhealthy* food and why it's important to choose healthy food.

 Count. Say. Trace.

11

12

Key Language: *How many (stars) can you see? Let's count. One, two, three, four, five, six, seven, eight, nine, ten, eleven, twelve.* Look at the first jacket and ask: *How many stars can you see? Let's count.* Count the eleven stars together, then point to number 11 and finger trace while repeating the number: *eleven, eleven, eleven.* Optional: Children trace the number. Repeat the process with the second jacket and number 12.

29

✏️ Draw. 💬 Say.

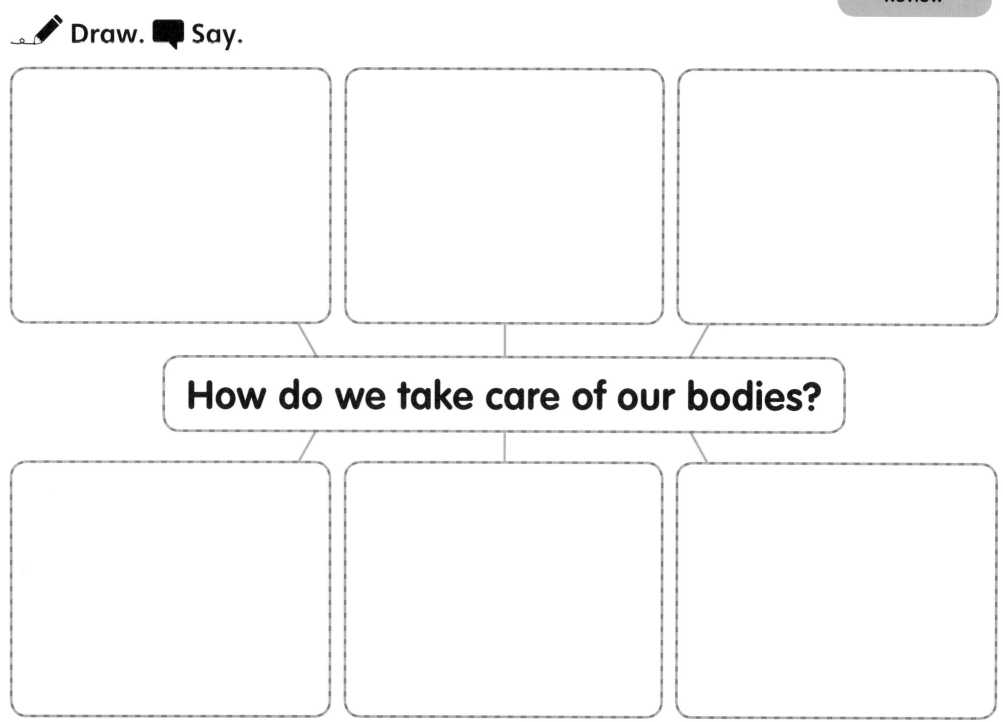

How do we take care of our bodies?

Key Language: *How do we take care of ourselves? I wash my face, brush my hair, eat healthy food, drink water, put on a jacket, toothbrush, brush, towel, soap, jump rope, I'm (tired, thirsty, hungry, dirty, sick). I can (sleep, take medicine).* Ask the Big Question: *How do we take care of ourselves?* Children look back through the unit to recall what they have learned. Then they draw six things they can do to take care of themselves, such as drink water, jump rope, sleep. Ask volunteers to share their drawings with the class and name what they drew. Finally, answer the Big Question together, using the children's drawings to help.

(3) What do we do at home?

 Say. ✂ Cut. ▌ Glue.

bedroom

bathroom

living room

dining room

kitchen

Key Language: *living room, dining room, kitchen, bedroom, bathroom.* Children look at the picture. Point to each room and each word, say the name and have children point and repeat after you. Distribute magazines, advertisements or pages of photos from the Internet. Children choose and cut out items to furnish the rooms, then glue them in the appropriate room. Children present their pages, naming the rooms, e.g., *This is the bedroom.* Optional: They trace the initial letter of the vocabulary items, while repeating the word.

💬 Say. ⭕ Circle. ✏️ Color.

A Fun Game

Key Language: *What / Who can you see? Where does the story take place? What happens in the story? Who are the characters?, door, water, candy.*
Children look at the story scenes. Ask the literacy questions. Then ask: *Can you see a door? Can you see water? Can you see candy?* Children circle and then color the items in the pictures.

🔲 Say. ⭕ Circle. ✏ Color.

Key Language: *What / Who can you see? What happens in the story?, candy, cat.* Children look at the story scenes. Ask the literacy questions. Then ask: *Can you see candy? Can you see a cat?* Children circle and then color the items in the pictures. Then they retell the story in their own words. Provide language as needed.

 **Say.** **Draw.** **Color.**

Do you like the story?

Key Language: *Can you remember? Is this a scene from the story? What's missing?* Children look at the scene. Say: *Can you remember? Is this a scene from the story?* Allow children to notice that the cat (Tabby) is missing. Ask: *What's missing?* Children describe the cat, where it is and what it is doing in the story (sleeping in its cat bed). Children draw the cat in the right place. Finally, ask: *Do you like the story? (Yes. / No.)* Children color the happy face or the sad face.

👁 Look. 💬 Say. ✏ Color.

Key Language: *How can we help at home?* Children look at the scene. Ask: *What are they doing? (Helping at home. Feeding the cat. Cleaning the floor.)* Then ask: *Are they helping at home? (Yes!)* Discuss why it is important to help at home. *(So our family is happy.)* Discuss what else we can do to help at home. *(Clean our bedrooms. Put toys away. Help prepare dinner, etc.)* Finally, children color the children who are helping at home.

35

 **Say.** **Count.** **Trace.**

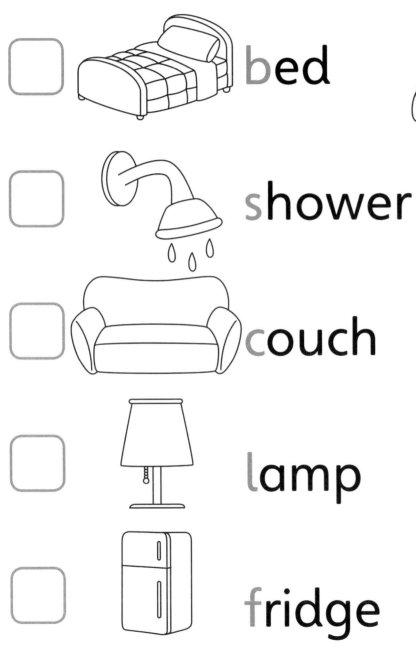

☐ **b**ed

☐ **s**hower

☐ **c**ouch

☐ **l**amp

☐ **f**ridge

Key Language: *shower, bed, couch, lamp, fridge.* Children look at the pictures on the left column and name each item. Then they search for each item inside the house and count them. Finally, say together, e.g., *How many beds? Three! Three beds.* Optional: Children write the number next to each item, with guidance. Optional: Then they trace the initial letter of each word.

👁 Look. ✏ Color. 💬 Say.

Key Language: *What's this? A (lamp / shower / bed / sofa / fridge). Where does it go? In the (kitchen / living room / bathroom / bedroom / dining room).*
The (bed) goes in the (bedroom). Look at the first room and name it together, then point to each item in the first row and ask: *What's this?* Children provide the
vocabulary. Then ask children to look at the pictures, choose and color the item that goes in each room. When they're finished, ask: *Where does it go?* and they say
where each item goes, e.g., *The shower goes in the bathroom.*

37

 **Say.** **Trace.**

in   under   on

Key Language: *on, in, under, Where's the (teddy bear)? The (teddy bear) is (in) the (bed).* Say: *Where's the teddy bear?* Then point to the picture of the bed and the word *in,* and say: *The teddy bear is in the bed!* Continue this way, saying: *The teddy bear is under the table* and *The teddy bear is on the sofa.* Optional: Children trace the initial letters of the words and say: *The teddy bear is ....*

 Look. Say. Trace.

 **s**weep the floor

 **c**ook

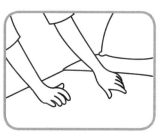 **m**ake the bed

 **s**et the table

 **w**atch TV

Key Language: *make the bed, sweep the floor, set the table, watch TV, cook, What does s/he do at home? S/he (cooks).* Children look at the pictures. Point to Leo and Mia's mom and ask: *What does she do at home?* Finger trace the line and then children say what she does at home: *She sweeps the floor.* Optional: children trace the initial letter of each word. Repeat with all the family members.

👁 Look. 💬 Say. ⭕ Circle.

Key Language: *What is s/he doing? S/he's (cook)ing. The (father)'s cooking. The (mother)'s making the bed.* Children look at the two scenes. Then they say what the people are doing in each scene, e.g., *Leo is making the bed.* Finally, children circle the differences in the second scene.

👁 Look. 💬 Say. ✏ Draw.

Key Language: *Where are you? I'm here! Where is Mia/Leo? S/he's here!* Children look at the scene and name the rooms. Explain Leo and Mia are playing a hiding game. Point to the first small picture and ask: *Where's Mia?* Children point to the corresponding location in the scene above and say: *She's here!* Continue with Leo and the other hiding places, asking the question and helping children with finding and answering. Then children draw a line from each character to the correct location in the scene and say, e.g., *Mia's here! She's in the kitchen.*

👁 Look. 💬 Say. ✏️ Color.

Key Language: *day, night, What do you do at home during the day / at night? I (play / sleep).* Ask: *What can you see?* Point to the sun and ask: *Day or night? Can you see the sun in the day or at night?* Continue with all the pictures, encouraging children to answer *Day* or *Night.* Finally, children color the day pictures yellow and the night pictures blue.

✋ Count. ⭕ Trace. ✏ Write.

13	14	15
13	14	15
13	14	15

 Draw. Say.

What do we do at home?

| Bedroom | Bathroom |

| Kitchen | Living Room |

Key Language: *bedroom, living room, dining room, kitchen, bathroom, shower, bed, couch, lamp, fridge, Do you help at home? What do you do at home?*
I cook / sweep the floor / set the table / watch TV / make the bed. Ask the Big Question: *What do we do at home?* Children look back through the unit to recall what
they have learned. Then they draw what they do or what they can see in each room, such as their bed, themselves in the kitchen setting the table, or in the living room
on the couch watching TV. Ask volunteers to share their drawings with the class. Finally, answer the Big Question together, using the children's drawings to help.

 **What can we see on a farm?**

👁 Look. ✏ Draw. ⭕ Trace.

horse

hen

cow

sheep

duck

Key Language: *cow, hen, duck, horse, sheep.* Show children the flashcard for each animal, saying the names as children repeat. Have them compare the flashcards to the pictures in their books. Children draw the missing part or parts of each animal, e.g., the tail on the cow. Optional: Children trace the initial letter of the word, while repeating the word.

45

🔲 **Say.** ⭕ **Circle.** ✏️ **Color.**

The Little Red Hen

Key Language: *What's the story about? What can you see? Who are the characters? Where does the story take place?* *hen, sheep, six, seeds.* Children look at the story scenes. Ask the literacy questions. Then ask: *Can you see a sheep? Can you see a hen? Can you see six seeds? Can you see a a hen planting?* Children circle, then color the items in the pictures.

🔊 Say. ○ Circle. ✏️ Color.

Key Language: *What's the story about? What can you see? Who are the characters? Where does the story take place? duck, yellow.* Children look at the story scenes. Ask the literacy questions. Then ask: *Can you see a duck? What color is the duck? (Yellow.)* Color the duck yellow. Children circle, then color the duck yellow in both pictures. Then they retell the story in their own words. Provide language as needed.

👆 Point. ◯ Circle. ✏ Color.

Do you like the story?

Key Language: *What happens first? What happens next? What happens at the end?* Ask children to remember the story and say: *What happens first?* Point to the first picture and retell together. Children trace or circle number 1. Then say: *What happens next?* pointing to the next picture, retelling together and tracing or circling number 2. Continue with the third and fourth picture and numbers. Finally, ask: *Do you like the story? (Yes. / No.)* Children color the happy face or the sad face.

👁 Look. 💬 Say. ✏ Color.

Key Language: *What is s/he doing? Is s/he working hard?* Children look at the scene. Ask: *What are they doing? (Working on the farm. Feeding the hens. Collecting eggs. Carrying water.)* Then ask: *Are they working hard on the farm? (Yes!)* Discuss why it is important to work hard. *(So everyone helps and everyone does their share.)* Finally, children color the people who are working hard on the farm.

 **Say.** **Match.** **Trace.**

milk the **c**ows

collect the **e**ggs

feed the **d**ucks

shear the **s**heep

groom the **h**orses

Key Language: *What do farmers do? feed the ducks, milk the cows, groom the horses, shear the sheep, collect the eggs.* Point to the farmer and ask: *What do farmers do?* Then point to the picture showing a pair of hands milking a cow and say: *Milk the cows.* as you finger trace a line between the action and the animal, the picture of the cow on the right. Children repeat and draw a line between the two pictures. Repeat for all the farmer's jobs. Optional: Children trace the initial letters of the words.

👁 Look. ✏🔲 Say. ✏ Color.

Key Language: *What is the farmer doing? He's milking the cow / shearing the sheep / collecting the eggs / feeding the ducks / grooming the horse.* Say a number between one and five. Children look at the corresponding picture and describe the farm chore: *The farmer collects the eggs.* Then they color the frame. Repeat until children have described all of the pictures.

51

👆 **Point.** 🗨 **Say.** ✏ **Draw.**

Key Language: *What comes next?* Children look at each row of animals. They point and say the name of each animal in the row. Guide the children to notice the pattern. Ask: *What comes next?* and help them with the responses by repeating the pattern, e.g., *Duck, cow, duck, cow, duck ... What comes next?* Then they draw the animal that completes the sequence.

🗨 Say. ➡➡ Follow. ⚪ Trace.

duckling   lamb   foal   chick   calf

Key Language: *calf, lamb, duckling, foal, chick.* Children look at the mother animals and name them: *duck, hen, horse, sheep, cow.* Then they follow the correct path with a crayon to the corresponding baby animal and say its name. Optional: Children trace the initial letters of the words.

✋ Count. ✏ Color. 💬 Say.

Key Language: *How many (cats) are there? There is one (cat). / There are two (cows).* Children look at the animals in the barn. Then they count the animals in each section and color the correct number. Finally, children say how many of each animal there are in the barn, e.g., *There is one cat in the barn. There are five ducklings in the barn.*

🗨 Say. 🖌 Paint.

What does a cow say?

Key Language: *What does a (cow / duck / hen / horse) say? moo, quack, cluck, neigh.* Point to a cow. Ask: *What does a cow say? (Moo, moo!)* Repeat with the remaining animals. Then have children paint the animals using finger paint or watercolors.

55

 **Say.** ○ **Circle.** ✏ **Color.**

Key Language: *Where does (milk / cheese / yogurt) come from? (Milk) comes from a (cow).* Point to the cheese and ask: *Where does cheese come from?*
Then point to the cow and say: *A cow!* Repeat with the other food and drink items. Children circle and color the food items we get from cows.

 Count. ✎ Color. ⭕ Trace.

16   17   18

Key Language: *How many (eggs) can you see? Let's count: one, two, three, four, five, six, seven, eight, nine, ten, eleven, twelve, thirteen, fourteen, fifteen, sixteen, seventeen, eighteen.* Point to the hen and explain that this hen has left a lot of eggs! Ask: *How many eggs?* Point to the number 16, say the number and have children repeat after you. Then lead the children in counting to 16. Say: *Let's count: one, two ... sixteen.* Children count 16 eggs below and color only 16 eggs. Repeat with 17 and 18. Optional: Children trace the numbers.

57

✏️ Draw. 💬 Say.

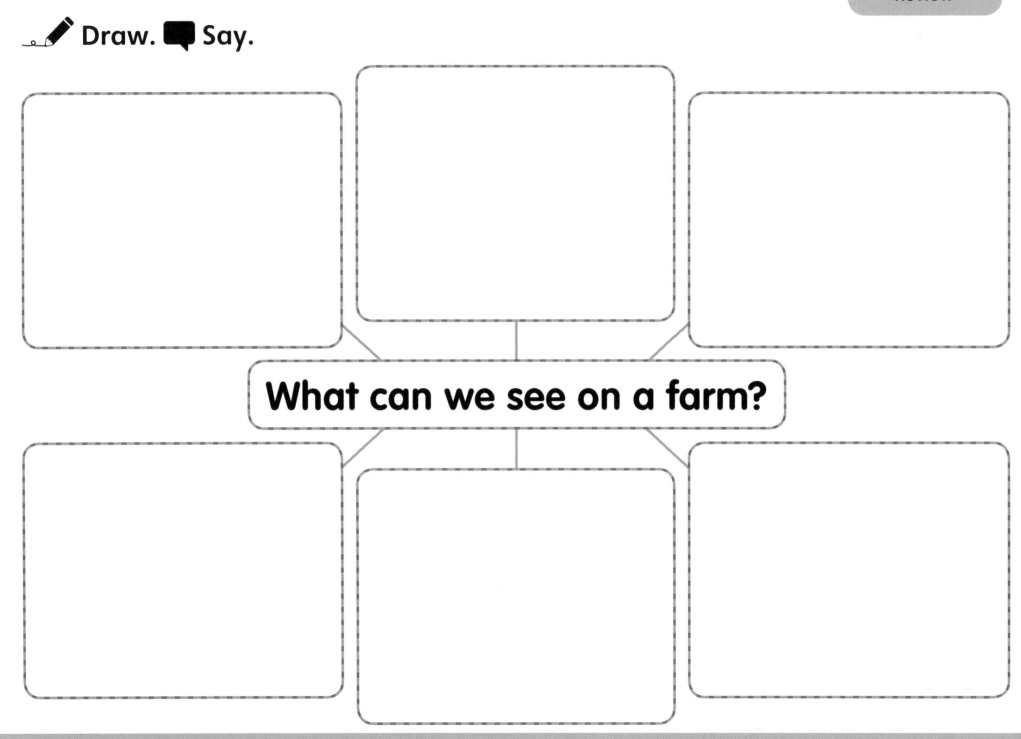

What can we see on a farm?

Key Language: *cow, hen, duck, horse, sheep, milk the cows, collect the eggs, groom the horses, feed the ducks, shear the sheep, calf, chick, duckling, foal, lamb, What is the farmer doing? The farmer's (milk)ing the (cow). Milk comes from cows. Eggs come from hens.* Ask the Big Question: *What can we see on a farm?* Children look back through the unit to recall what they have learned. Then they draw six things we can see on a farm, such as their favorite farm animals, a farmer feeding the hens, or some eggs. Ask volunteers to share their drawings with the class. Finally, answer the Big Question together, using the children's drawings to help.

 What do we eat at different times of the day?

🗨 Say. ✏ Draw. ⬭ Trace.

breakfast

lunch

dinner

eggs

chicken

salad

Key Language: *breakfast, lunch, dinner, eggs, chicken, salad.* Children point to the scenes and name the different meals: *breakfast, lunch, dinner.* Then ask them to listen carefully and draw eggs, chicken, and salad on the corresponding plates. Optional: Children trace the words.

59

■ Say. ○ Circle. ✎ Color.

Pat's Birthday Dream

Key Language: *What's the story about? What can you see? Who are the characters? Where does the story take place? Pat, sad.* Children look at the story scenes. Ask the literacy questions. Then ask: *Can you see Mom? Can you see Pat? Can you see someone who feels sad?* Children circle and then color the items in the pictures.

🗨 Say. ⭕ Circle. ✏ Color.

Key Language: *What's the story about? What can you see? Who are the characters? Where does the story take place? Pat, lunch, dinner.* Children look at the story scenes. Ask the literacy questions. Then ask: *Can you see lunch? Can you see dinner? Can you see ice cream?* Children circle and color the items in the pictures. Then they retell the story in their own words. Provide language as needed.

61

👁 Look. 💬 Say. ✏ Color.

Do you like the story?

Key Language: *Can you remember? Is this in the story? Is it real or a dream?* Point at the first picture showing Pat's surprise party and say: *Can you remember? Is this in the story? (Yes!)* Repeat with the picture of Pat dreaming of a cupcake and guide the children to answer *No.* Then go back to the first picture and ask: *Is this real? Or is it a dream? (It's real.)* Continue with the second picture and guide children to answer *It's a dream.* Encourage them to give you examples of things they have dreamed about and discuss the difference between reality and dreams. Finally, ask: *Do you like the story? (Yes. / No.)* Children color the happy face or the sad face.

👁 Look. 💬 Say. ✏ Color.

Key Language: *a healthy breakfast, energy.* Children look at the scene and describe it. Ask: *What is she doing? (Eating breakfast. Eating a meal.)* Then ask: *Is she eating a healthy breakfast? (Yes!)* Discuss why it is important to eat a healthy breakfast. *(So we have energy to learn and play.)* Finally, children color the healthy breakfast items.

 Say. Color. Trace.

water

pancakes

soup

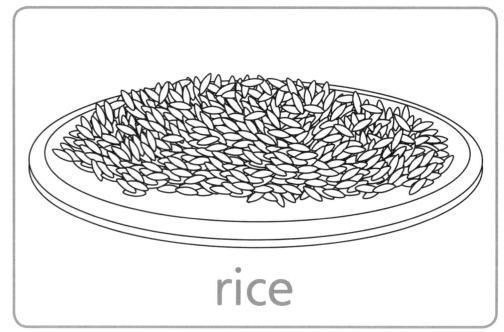

rice

Key Language: *water, pancakes, soup, rice.* Children look at each picture and name the food item. Then they color the items they like.
Optional: Children trace the words.

🗨 Say. ⊞ Play.

Key Language: *What do you like? I like (bananas). I don't like (pizza).* Tell children you are going to play a game. Throw the dice, say the number, count the number of spaces and say *I like/don't like (fish).* to demonstrate. Explain that the snakes and ladders are very special. If you land by a ladder, you climb to the picture it leads to. If you land by a snake, you slide down to the picture it leads to! Children take turns playing and continue until they reach the finish line.

65

👁 Look. ⭕ Circle. 🗨 Say.

Key Language: *How many (apples)? There are a few (apples)/ There are a lot of (pancakes).* Children look at the pictures. In each picture, children decide whether there are a few or a lot. If there are only a few, children circle the items. Finally, they point to each and say, e.g., *He has a lot of apples. She has a few pancakes.*

 Say. ✏ Color. ⚪ Trace.

	☀ (sunrise)	☀ (sun)	☾ (moon and stars)
milk			
orange juice			
cereal			
fish			
strawberries			

Key Language: *milk, orange juice, cereal, fish, strawberries.* Point to the three pictures across the top and explain that they show different times of day when we eat our meals. Elicit which represents *breakfast, lunch* and *dinner.* Children look at the food and drinks and name each. They then think about when they eat or drink that item and color in the blank spaces accordingly. Point out that they can color more than one space if, for example, they drink milk at breakfast and also at dinner. Optional: Children trace the words.

67

◯ Trace. ✏ Draw. 🔲 Say.

yellow

orange

blue

Key Language: *I have (eggs) for breakfast. I have (fish and rice) for dinner.* Point to the pictures across the top row and discuss what times of day they represent. Distribute yellow, orange and blue crayons. Children color the crayons in the color indicated. Then they trace each place mat in one of those colors to represent the three meals we eat at different times of day. Children draw and color what they eat and drink in the morning, in the afternoon, and in the evening. Finally, children describe their meals: *I have breakfast in the morning. I have cereal and strawberries. I have milk.*

👁 Look. 🗨 Say. ✏ Color.

Key Language: *What do you want for breakfast / lunch? (Pancakes / Chicken and milk / Juice), please.* Children look at the pictures. Ask: *What does Leo want for breakfast? (Pancakes and milk.) What does Mia want for lunch? (Chicken, rice, salad, and juice.)* Tell children they are going to pretend to be Leo or Mia. Each child chooses. Then role play, asking: *What's your name? (Mia) What do you want for lunch, Mia? (Chicken and rice, please!)* Continue until all children have had a turn. Then children color the meal that they wanted.

 **Say.** **Draw.** **Color.**

Key Language: *Does (milk) come from (cows)? (Eggs) come from (hens).* Ask children to look at the food items and name them. Then they name the animals. Return to the first food item and ask: *Do eggs come from cows? Do eggs come from hens?* Elicit answers. Children draw a line from the egg to the hen. Continue with all the food items, with children drawing other lines where appropriate. Finally, children color the food items that come from the animals as well as the animals.

 Count. Trace. Say.

17

18

19

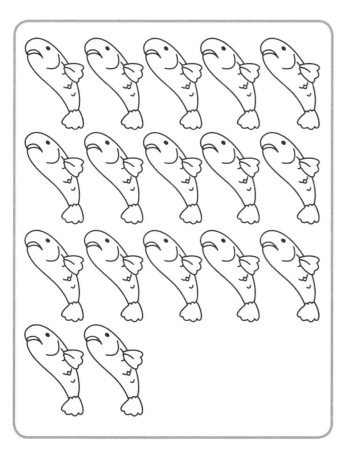

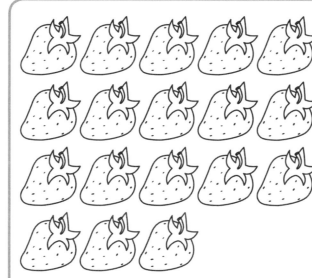

Key Language: *How many (fish) can you see? Let's count: one, two, three, four, five, six, seven, eight, nine, ten, eleven, twelve, thirteen, fourteen, fifteen, sixteen, seventeen, eighteen, nineteen.* Look at the group of fish. Ask: *How many fish can you see? Let's count.* Count together up to 17. Children trace or circle the number 17 above. Then they say: *Seventeen, seventeen fish.* Optional: children color the seventeen fish. Repeat for the 18 strawberries and 19 eggs.

 Draw. Say.

What do we eat at different times of the day?

Breakfast	Lunch	Dinner

Key Language: *breakfast, lunch, dinner, eggs, chicken, salad, water, rice, soup, pancakes, milk, orange juice, cereal, fish, strawberries, What food do you like? I like (pancakes). I don't like (eggs). What food does s/he like? S/he likes (rice). S/he doesn't like (salad). I have (milk) for breakfast. I have (soup) for lunch.* Ask the Big Question: *What do we eat at different times of the day?* Children look back through the unit to recall what they have learned. Then they draw foods and drinks they have for each meal. Ask volunteers to share their drawings with the class. Finally, answer the Big Question, using the children's drawings to help.

 **What different kinds of clothes do we wear?**

🗨 Say. ▮ Glue ⬭ Trace.

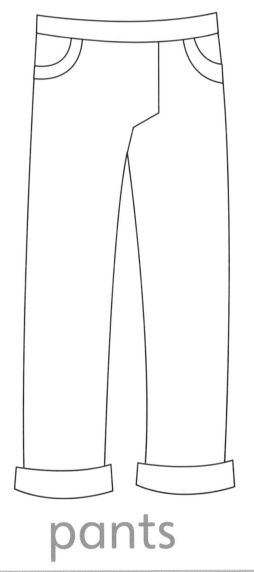

shoes

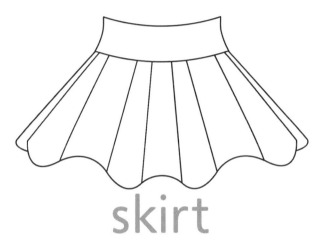

skirt

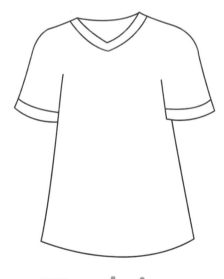

pants

T-shirt

sweater

Key Language: *pants, shoes, T-shirt, skirt, sweater.* Point to each item of clothing and ask children to name it. Then point to items the children are wearing and name them. Add a color, e.g., *Look, a blue T-shirt. Green pants.* encouraging children to repeat and participate. Explain they are going to add color to the clothes on the page. Cut small squares of different colored tissue paper: red, blue, yellow, green, orange. Children glue the squares of blue paper on the pants, red on the shoes, yellow on the T-shirt, green on the skirt, and orange on the sweater. Then they point to each and say, e.g., *Blue pants. A yellow T-shirt.* Optional: Children trace the words.

73

■ Say. ○ Circle. ✎ Color.

The Teddy Bear Show

Key Language: *What can you see? What's the story about? Who are the characters? wig, teddy bear.* Children look at the story scenes. Ask the literacy questions. Then ask: *Can you see a wig on a teddy bear? Can you see a big teddy bear?* Children circle and then color the items in the pictures.

🗨 Say. ⭕ Circle. ✏ Color.

Key Language: *What can you see? What's the story about? Who are the characters? teddy bear, skirt, clothes.* Children look at the story scenes. Ask the literacy questions. Then ask: *Can you see a teddy bear wearing a skirt? Can you see a teddy bear wearing super clothes?* Children circle and then color the items in the pictures. Then they retell the story in their own words. Provide language as needed.

75

 Draw. Color. Say.

Do you like the story?

Key Language: *Can you remember? What are the characters wearing?* Ask the class to look at the children and teddy bears from the story. Ask: *Can you remember? What are they wearing?* Elicit ideas and check if necessary. Children draw the clothing items onto the characters in the story. Then they color the pictures. Finally, ask: *Do you like the story? (Yes. / No.)* Children color the happy face or the sad face.

 Look. 💬 Say. ✏ Color.

Key Language: *Take care of our clothes. hang up.* Children look at the scene and describe it. Ask: *What is he doing? (Hanging up his clothes.)* Then ask: *Is he taking care of his clothes? (Yes!)* Discuss why it is important to take care of our clothes. *(So they look nice and clean and to help our family.)* Finally, children color the boy and the clothes he is taking care of.

🗨 Say. ✏ Color. ⭕ Trace.

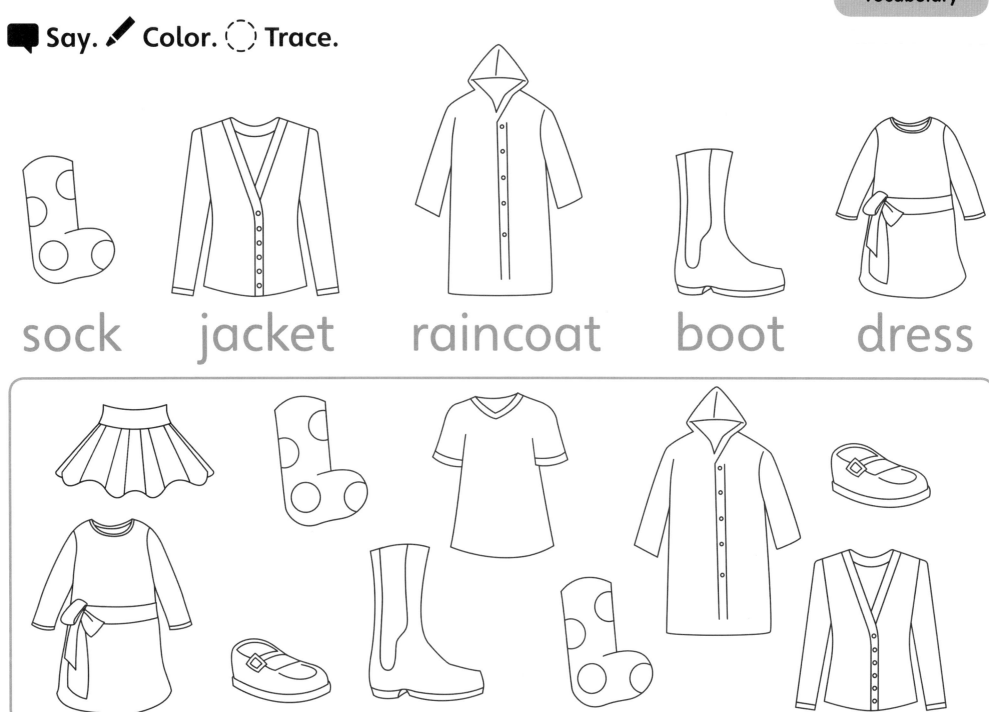

sock　　jacket　　raincoat　　boot　　dress

Key Language: *socks, jacket, boots, raincoat, dress.* Look and point at each clothing item as children name them. Return to the first item (sock) and ask: *Can you find the socks? Color the socks.* Repeat for the remaining 4 items, suggesting children use a different color for each different clothing item and making sure they color only the items that appear at the top of the page (socks, jackets, raincoats, boots and dress). Optional: Children trace the words as they say them.

✏️ Color. 💬 Say.

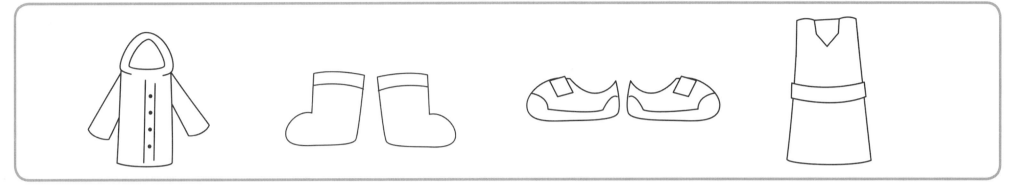

Key Language: *What color is the (raincoat)? What color are the (shoes)? What is s/he wearing? S/he's wearing (a yellow raincoat and red boots).* Point to each clothing item across the top as children name them. Then distribute crayons. Explain that children must ask about the clothes, e.g., *What color is the (dress)? What color are the (shoes)?* and you will answer e.g., *The (dress) is (purple). The (shoes) are (black).* Children listen and color the items. Then they color the children's clothes according to the key. Finally, they share their coloring and take turns describing the children, saying, e.g. *She's wearing a purple dress and black shoes.*

▮ Match. ✎ Color. ▮ Say.

Left ⇦

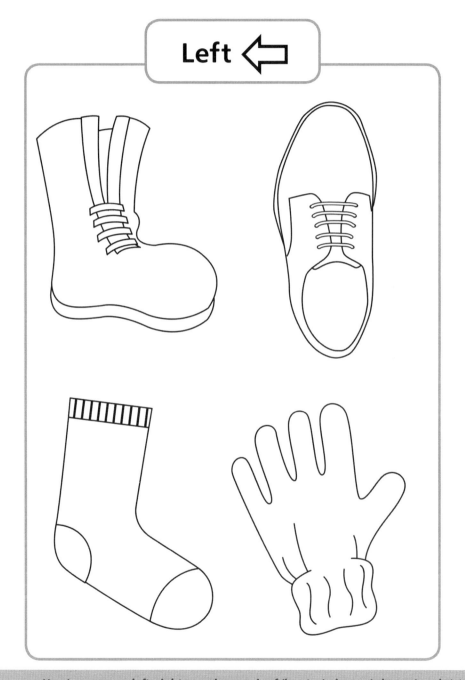

⇨ Right

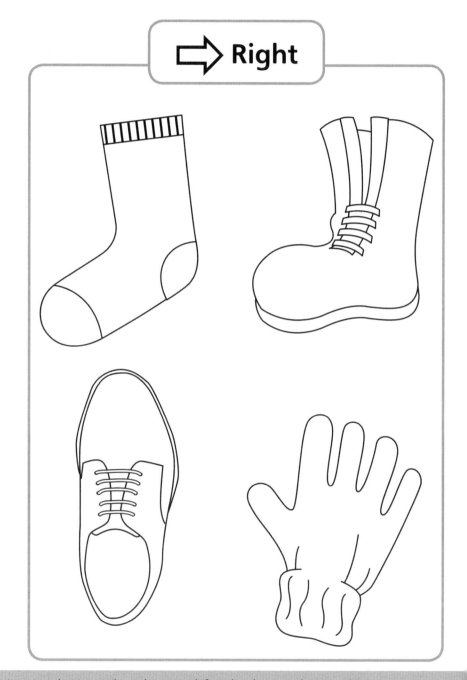

Key Language: *left, right, a pair, a pair of (boots / gloves / shoes / socks).* Look at the clothing items and point out how there are *left* and *right* items that together make a pair. Children draw lines to match the items to make pairs. Then they color the pairs in the same color, i.e., both socks green, both boots orange. Finally, they finger trace between them saying, e.g., *A pair of boots, left and right. A pair of shoes, left and right.* etc.

 Say. ✏ Color. ◯ Trace.

sunny

snowy

cloudy

windy

rainy

Key Language: *What's the weather like? sunny, snowy, cloudy, windy, rainy*. Look at each window and ask children: *What's the weather like?* Children answer and then color the weather inside each window. Optional: Children trace the words and say them aloud.

👁 Look. ⭕ Circle. 🔲 Say.

Key Language: *What's the weather like? What's (Mia / Leo) wearing? S/he's wearing ...* Point to each weather picture and ask: *What's the weather like?* Once they have answered, point to the characters and ask: *What's Mia / Leo wearing?* Explain they should circle the character wearing the appropriate clothes. Finally, children say what the weather is like and what each appropriately dressed child is wearing, e.g., *It's snowy. Leo is wearing a jacket and boots.*

 Look. Draw. Say.

What's the weather like?

It's rainy.

It's cold.

Key Language: *What's the weather like today? It's (rainy). Put on your (raincoat)!* Point to each picture and ask: *What's the weather like?* Children respond: *It's rainy. It's snowy.* They they look and think about what the characters should be wearing. Model first and children repeat after you: *Put on your raincoat / jacket!* Children draw the appropriate clothes for each character. Finally, they say, e.g., *It's rainy. Mia's wearing a raincoat. It's snowy. Leo's wearing a jacket.*

83

✏ Color. 💬 Say.

Spring

Summer

Fall

Winter

Key Language: *seasons, spring, summer, fall, winter.* Point to each season's picture and ask children to name the season. Then complete the color code. Say a number and have children color that crayon accordingly, e.g., 1. red, 2. yellow, 3. green, 4. blue, 5. brown, 6. orange, 7. white. Then children color the scenes by number. Finally, ask children to describe how they've colored their pictures by using the seasons vocabulary, e.g., *Winter is blue and red. Fall is green and brown. Spring is pink and yellow!*

👁 Look. ✋ Count. ✏ Color.

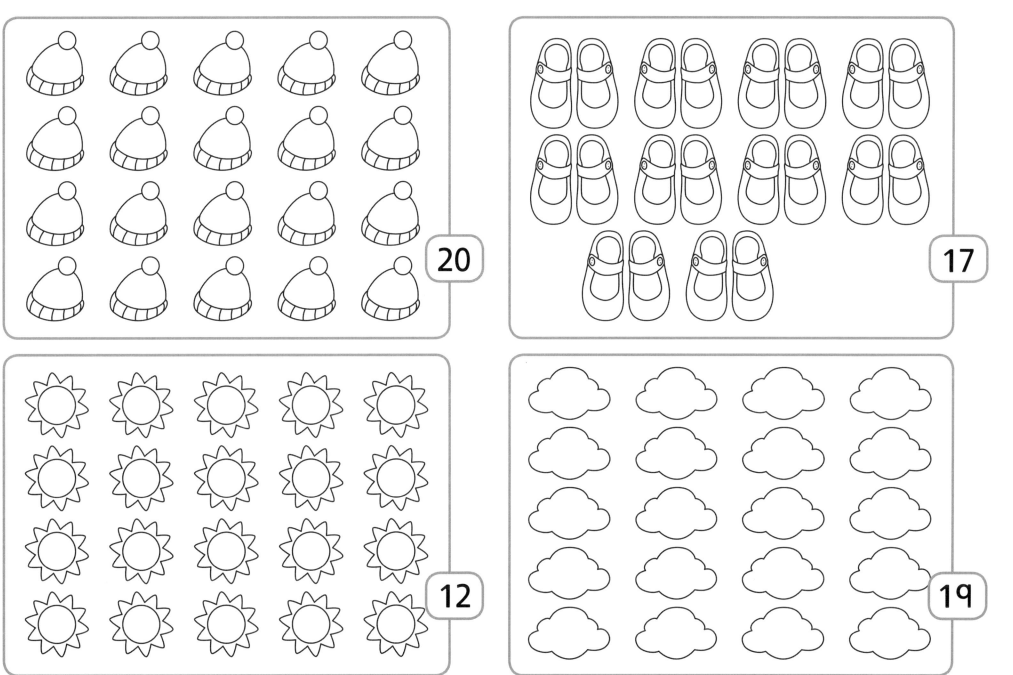

20

17

12

19

Key Language: *How many (hats) can you see? Let's count: one, two … nineteen, twenty.* Children look at the numbers, count, and color the corresponding number of items in each section.

85

 **Draw.** **Say.**

What different kinds of clothes do we wear?

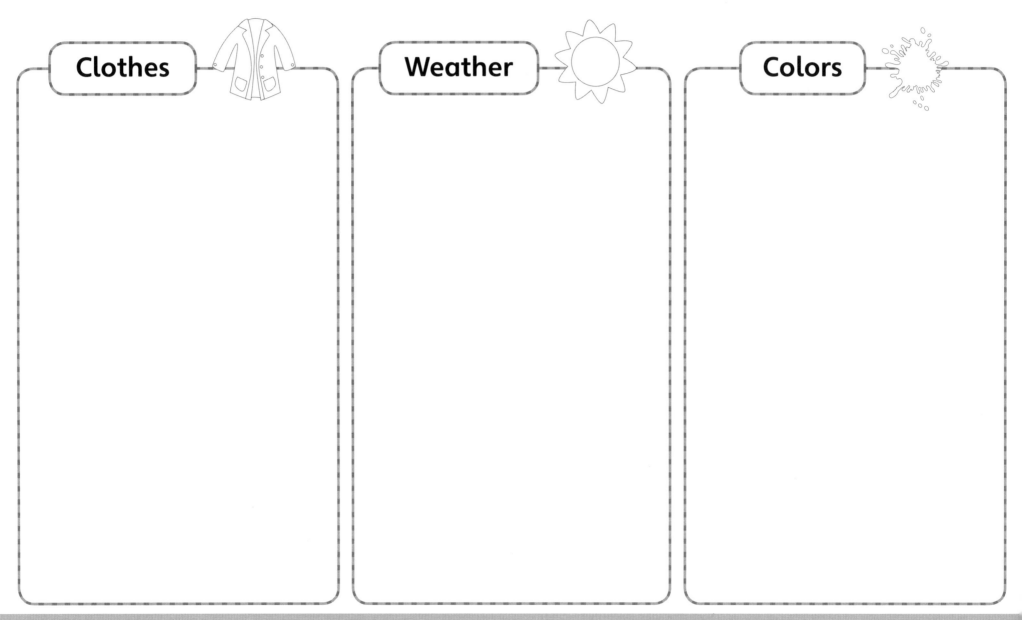

Clothes	Weather	Colors

Key Language: *pants, shoes, T-shirt, skirt, sweater, socks, jacket, boots, raincoat, dress, What is s/he wearing? S/he's wearing a (blue) ... What are you wearing? I'm wearing (yellow) ... I put on my (socks.) What's the weather like? sunny, windy, snowy, rainy, cloudy, Put on your (jacket)! seasons, spring, summer, fall, winter.* Ask the Big Question: *What different kinds of clothes do we wear?* Children look back through the unit to recall what they have learned. Then they draw what they remember under the correct heading. Ask volunteers to share their drawings with the class, answering the Big Question together.

7 What can we do with our senses?

🗨 Say. 📖 Match. ⭕ Trace.

see

touch

hear

smell

taste

Key Language: *see, touch, hear, smell, taste.* Ask children to look at the page and name each sense. Ask them to point to the same body part on their own bodies while saying the word, e.g., they point at their noses and say *smell.* Then they draw lines between the sense picture and the same body part on the girl. They finger trace the lines first, repeating the word, e.g., *see-see,* and then draw them with a pencil. Optional: Children trace the words.

■ Say. ○ Circle. ✎ Color.

The Apple Pie

Key Language: *What can you see? What's the story about? Who are the characters? Where does the story take place? cut, sun.* Children look at the story scenes. Ask the literacy questions. Then ask: *Can you see the sun? Can you see apples? Can you see apples cut in half?* Children circle and then color the items in the pictures.

88

Say. ○ Circle. ✏ Color.

Key Language: *What can you see? What's the story about? Who are the characters? Where does the story take place? smell, look.* Children look at the story scenes. Ask the literacy questions. Then ask: *Can you see anyone smelling the pie? Can you see anyone looking at the pie?* Children circle and then color the characters who are using their senses in the pictures. Then they retell the story in their own words. Provide language as needed.

👁 Look. 💬 Say. ✏ Color.

Do you like the story?

Key Language: *Can you remember? Is this a scene from the story?* Children look at the scenes. Point to each scene and ask: *Is this scene from the story? (Yes. / No.)* Children color the frames of the scenes from the story. Finally, ask: *Do you like the story? (Yes. / No.)* Children color the happy face or the sad face.

🗨 Say. ✏ Draw. ✏ Color.

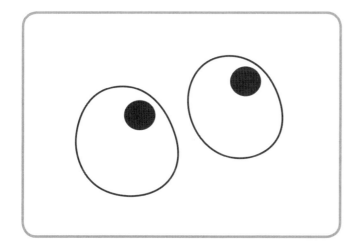 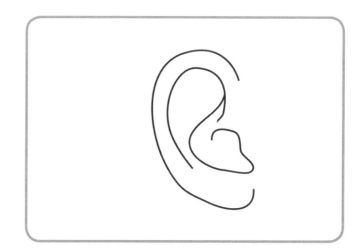

Key Language: *S/he can't see well. S/he can't hear well. We're all different!* Look at the pictures of the three children together. Point to the boy and ask: *Can he see well? (No.)* Explain that some people can't see very well but wearing glasses helps them to see. Children draw a line from the boy to the eyes. Continue with the other children, explaining in turn how wearing a hearing aid and glasses helps them hear and see better. When they have finished, they color the three children. Discuss how everyone is different. Ask children if they know other ways we are different from each other. Discuss how it is important to respect these differences.

91

 **Say.** **Color.** **Trace.**

	good	🌹 🍰 🚗
	bad	📦 🗑️
	soft	🧸 🪑
	rough	🧱 🪵 🛏️
	smooth	🪑 🍎 🧈

Key Language: *How does it feel / smell? soft, rough, smooth, good, bad.* Point to the picture of the nose, sniff a little bit and ask: *How does it smell?* Point to the good picture and children answer: *Good!* Children color only the picture(s) in the row that smell good (rose, cake). Repeat with *bad* (trash). Then continue below, pointing to the hand, touching a smooth table top and asking: *How does it feel?* and eliciting the answers (*soft:* teddy, *rough:* bricks, wood, *smooth:* table, apple). Again children color the representative pictures. Optional: Children trace the words.

 Look. 💬 Say.

Key Language: *It smells good/bad. It feels rough/soft.* Children place a crayon in the middle of the circle, spin it, and look at the picture where it stops. Then they decide if it is something we feel or smell and say what the item smells or feels like, e.g., *A cookie smells good. A lamb feels soft.*

 **Look.** 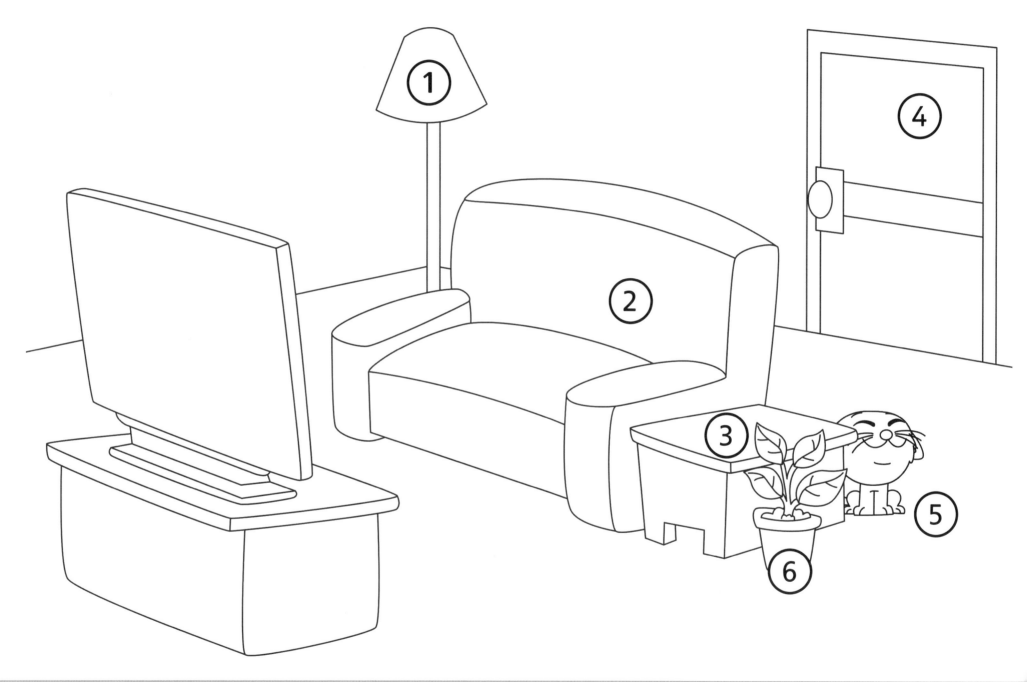 **Say.** ✏️ **Draw.**

Key Language: *Where's (Tickles)? Next to / between / behind the (table). (Tickles) is behind the (table). The (couch) is between the (lamp) and the (table).*
Call out a number from one to six. Children look for the object in the picture with that number and name the object. Continue until you have called all the numbers. Then ask about the position of random objects, e.g., *Where is Tickles?* Children respond using the language, e.g., *Tickles is behind the table.* Finally, children draw a picture of a ball somewhere they choose in the scene. Go around to each child asking: *Where's the ball?* and children respond.

 **Say.** ✏ **Color.** ⬭ **Trace.**

	loud	salty	sweet	beautiful	soft

Key Language: *How does it taste / sound / look? Sweet, salty, loud, quiet, beautiful.* Point to the picture of the eyes and ask: *How does it look?* Point to each picture in the top row and ask: *Loud? (No.) Salty? (No.) Sweet? (No.) Beautiful? (Yes!)* Children color in the section below *beautiful.* Repeat with the mouth and ear, asking: *How does it taste / sound?* as children think and color in the correct sections. Optional: Children trace the words.

🔲 Say. ⭕ Trace. 🔲 Say.

Key Language: *How does it (sound / feel / look / smell / taste)? It (sounds / feels / looks / smells / tastes) (sweet / salty / loud / quiet / beautiful / soft / smooth / rough / good / bad). I need my ears / hands / eyes / nose / mouth.* Children look at each picture and ask the appropriate question: *How does it ...?* Then, they trace the line from each sense or body part to the object at the bottom of the page. Finally, children describe the object and say what sense they need to perceive it, e.g., *It sounds loud. I need my ears.*

 Look. Draw. Say.

It tastes sweet

It tastes salty

Key Language: *How does it taste? It tastes sweet / salty.* Point to Mia and finger trace the line to the lollipop, asking: *How does it taste?* Elicit the answer: *It tastes sweet.* Then repeat with Leo, finger tracing to the cheese and eliciting: *It tastes salty.* Children draw lines from Mia to the other sweet foods and from Leo to the other salty foods. Finally, point to each item and ask children: *How does it taste?*

 Look. 💬 Say. ✏️ Color.

The Five Senses

Key Language: *Which sense is it? Can you hear / smell / see / taste / touch it?* Point to each body part in the first column and ask children: *Which sense is it?* Children name the five senses. Children look at the picture of the first item in the top row (the guitar). Ask: *Can you see / hear / smell / taste / touch a guitar?* Children color in the section next to the senses we use to perceive a guitar. Repeat with the remaining items. Finally, children say how they can perceive each item, e.g., *I can see a guitar. I can hear a train.*

 Color. ✋ Count. ◯ Trace.

| 10 | 20 | 30 |

Key Language: *How many (petals) can you see? Let's count: one, two, three, four, five, six, seven, eight, nine, ten. Ten, twenty, thirty. Set of ten. Three sets of ten.* Distribute crayons in three colors. Children color the flowers different colors. Then ask: *How many petals on the flowers?* Point to the first flower on the left and say: *Let's count.* Count to 10 together. Continue with the other two flowers. Then say: *How many sets of ten? Three. How many petals? Let's count by tens: Ten, twenty, thirty!* Optional: Children trace the numbers and repeat them.

 Draw. 💬 Say.

What can we do with our senses?

See 👀

Touch ✋

Hear 👂

Smell 👃

Taste 👄

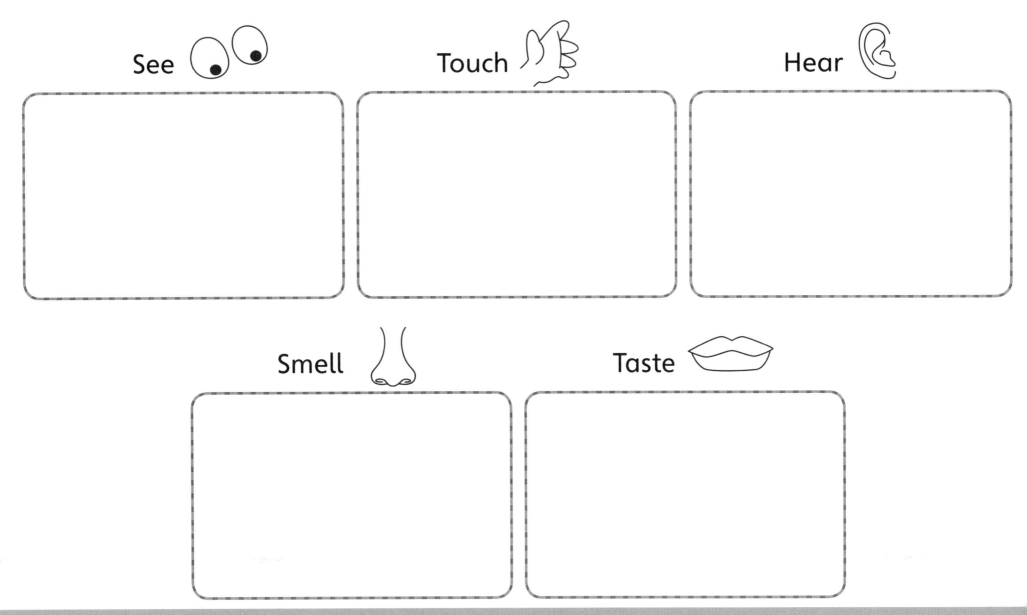

Key Language: *senses, see, touch, hear, smell, taste, How does it feel / smell? It feels soft / rough / smooth. It smells good / bad. How does it taste / sound / look? It tastes sweet / salty. It sounds loud / quiet. It looks beautiful.* Ask the Big Question: *What can we do with our senses?* Children look back through the unit to recall what they have learned. Then they draw an example of what they can perceive with each of their five senses. Ask volunteers to share their drawings with the class and describe what they drew. Finally, answer the Big Question together, using the children's drawings to help.

8 How do we get from one place to another?

✏ Color. 🔲 Say. ⭕ Trace.

plane ④

boat ⑤

car ①

train ②

bus ③

1
2
3
4
5

Key Language: *car, train, bus, airplane, boat.* Point to the crayon pictures, distribute crayons to children and explain they are going to color the crayons to make a code. Say: *One. Color number 1 red. Two. Color number 2 blue. Three. Color number 3 yellow. Four. Color number four green. Five. Color number five orange.* Next children look at the vehicles and use the color code to color them the corresponding color. Finally, they point to each and say: *It's a boat. An orange boat. It's a plane. A green plane.* and so on. Optional: Children trace the words.

🗨 Say. ◯ Circle. ✏ Color.

Let's Climb a Mountain!

Key Language: *What can you see? What's the story about? Who are the characters? What are they doing? Where does the story take place?, Bob, top, mountain, train, bus.* Children look at the story scenes. Ask the literacy questions. Then ask: *Can you see a train? Can you see a bus? Can you see Bob? Can you see the top of the mountain?* Children circle and then color the items in the pictures.

Say. ○ Circle. ✎ Color.

Key Language: *What can you see? What's the story about? Who are the characters? What are they doing? Where does the story take place? top, plain, mountain.* Children look at the story scenes. Ask the literacy questions. Then ask: *Can you see a plane? Can you see the children at the top of the mountain?* Children circle and then color the items in the pictures. Then they retell the story in their own words. Provide language as needed.

103

 **Say.** ✏ **Color.**

Do you like the story?

Key Language: *Do you remember? Is it in the story? Is it real or imaginary?* Ask children to remember the story. Then ask them to look at the images on the page. Point to the first picture and ask: *Is this in the story? Is it real or is it imaginary?* Elicit the answer *(Real.)* Explain that this did happen in the story, that the kids did play on the swings, so that makes it real. Continue in this way with the other two pictures, guiding children into deciding whether each scene is real or imaginary. When they have finished, children color only the images that are real. Finally, ask: *Do you like the story? (Yes. / No.)* Children color the happy face or the sad face.

 **Look.** **Say.** **Color.**

Key Language: *take care of the air, Taking a (bike / scooter) keeps the air clean. Planting trees keeps the air clean.* Children look at the scene and describe it. Ask: *What are they doing? (Planting a tree in the park.)* Then ask: *Are they taking care of the air? (Yes!) Are they keeping the air clean? (Yes!)* Explain that trees help to clean the air. Discuss why it is important to take care of the air. (So we have a beautiful and healthy environment and we don't get sick.) Finally, children color the children who are taking care of the air by planting the tree.

■ Say. ◯ Trace. ✏ Color.

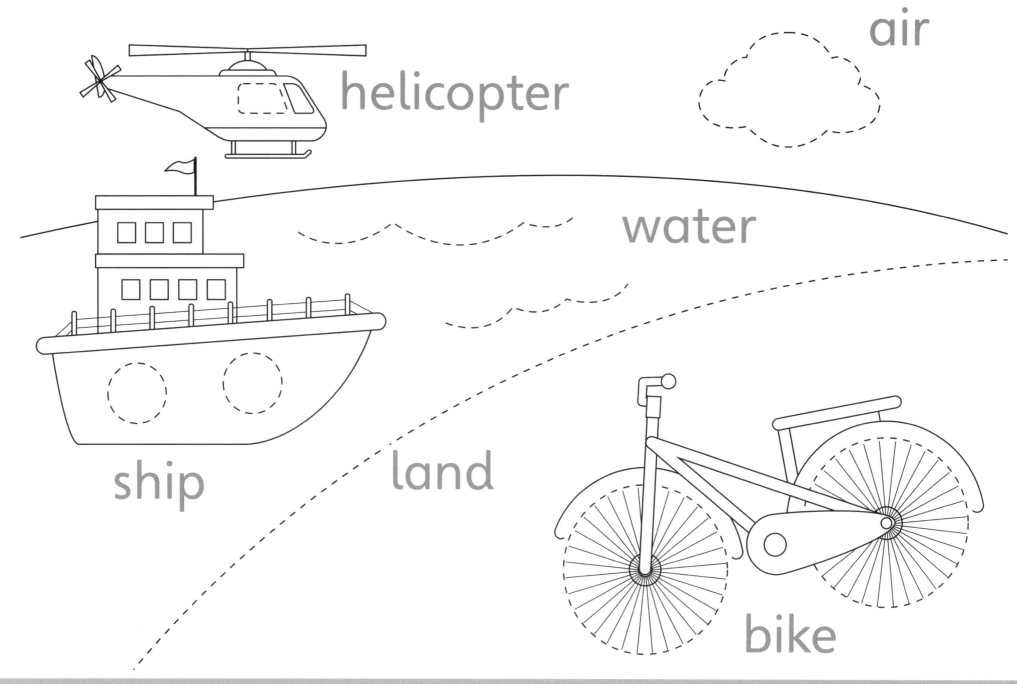

helicopter

air

water

ship

land

bike

Key Language: *bike, helicopter, ship, air, water, land.* Children look at the pictures and name the items. Then they trace the shoreline, waves, the windows on the boat and helicopter, the wheels on the bike and the cloud and color the pictures. Optional: Children trace the words.

👁 Look. ✏ Color. 💬 Say.

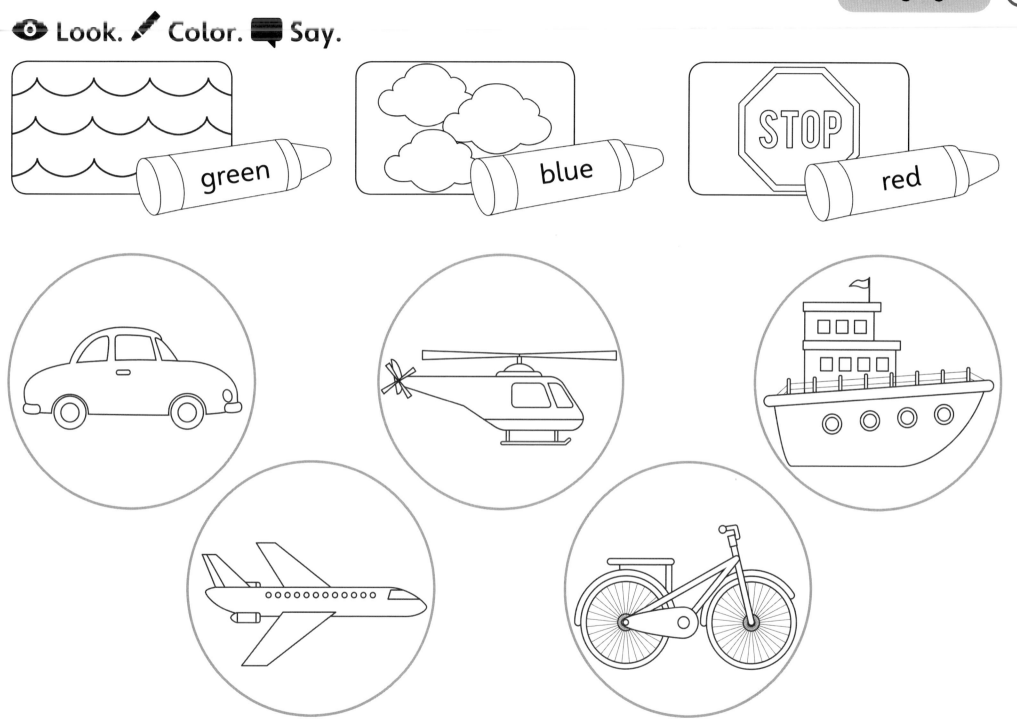

green

blue

red

Key Language: *Where does a (bus) go? On land / In the air / In the water. A (bus) goes (on land).* Distribute crayons in green, blue and red. Tell children to color the three crayons on the page in the corresponding color. When they're finished, point to each picture next to a crayon and ask children what it represents, e.g., *Is this water, air or land?* Elicit the answers. Then point the images of vehicles and tell the children that they're going to color them following the color key they have just prepared. Point to each vehicle and ask, e.g., *Where does a car go?* Elicit the answer and have children color. Finally, children point and say: *This is a car. A car goes on land.*

◯ Circle. 👆 Point. 🔲 Say.

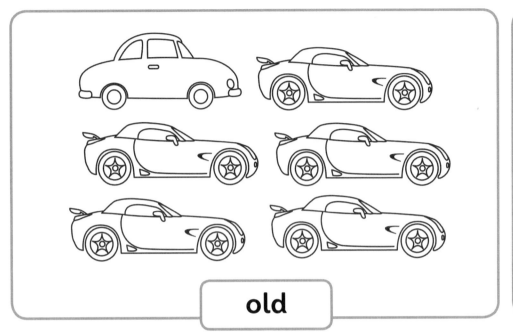

old

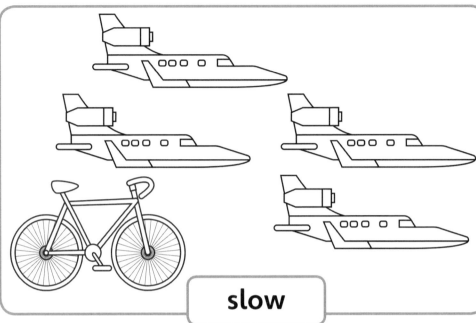

slow

new

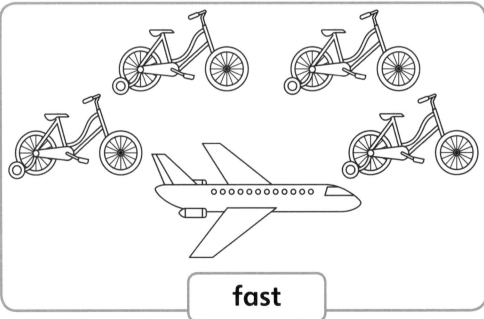

fast

Key Language: *new, old, slow, fast, This (car) is new / old. This (plane) is slow / fast.* Children look at the pictures in each section. Then they circle the picture that is different. Finally, children point and say why it's different, e.g., *This car is old.*

 Say. Color. Draw.

beach   amusement park   mountains   city

Key Language: *beach, amusement park, mountains, city.* Children look at the pictures. They name each place and color the box if they have been to that place. Finally, children draw their favorite place. Optional: Children trace the words.

109

◉ Look. ✏ Draw. 🗩 Say.

Key Language: *Where is s/he going? S/he's going to the (city). How is s/he going to get there? S/he's going to get there (in a car).* Children look at each maze. Point to the pictures that show a character in turn and ask: *Where is s/he going?* Children draw a path to the end of the maze with a crayon. Finally, return to each character and ask again: *Where is s/he going?* Then ask: *How is s/he going to get there?* Children reply using the vocabulary and structures, e.g., *He's going to a city. He's going to get there on an airplane.*

 Draw. Color. Say.

This is a train.	This is a boat.
This is a car.	This is an airplane.

Key Language: *This is my (train). It's fast / slow / old / new / red / yellow ...* Read the phrases in each box and ask children to draw the type of transportation in the box, making the vehicles look old or new, slow or fast and using colors of their choice. Finally, children present one of their drawings to the class using the vocabulary and structures, e.g., *This is my (train). It's (fast). It's (red).* Optional: Children trace the words.

✏ Paint. ✏ Color. 💬 Say.

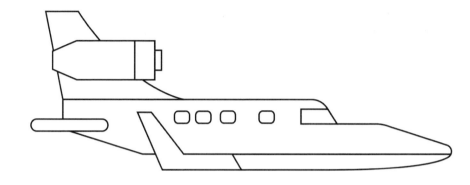

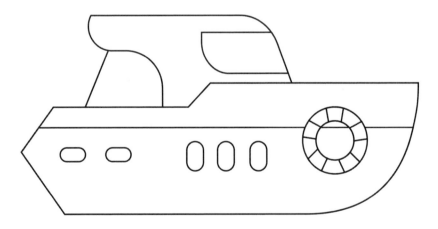

Key Language: *This is a boat. It's green. It goes on water. It's fast.* Point to the plane and ask: *Where does it go? (In the air.)* Repeat with the boat, eliciting the answer: *In the water.* Distribute watercolors or finger paint. Children create the sky (air) and the water with the paint. Encourage them to use different colors and different lines (wavy lines for the water, straight lines for the sky) to create different effects. Then they complete the picture by coloring the vehicles using crayons. Finally, they present their pages using the language from the unit, e.g., *This is a plane. It goes in the air. It's fast. It's red.*

 Count. Draw. Trace.

10   20   30   40

Key Language: *How many (clouds) can you see? Let's count by tens, ten, twenty, thirty, forty. There are four sets of ten.* Point to the first frame and ask: *How many clouds? Let's count.* Count to 10 together. Explain that children must draw 10 more clouds in the next frame. When they're finished, ask: *Now how many clouds? Let's count by tens: Ten, twenty!* Repeat with the remaining two frames, children drawing 10 more clouds each time and counting by tens together. Optional: Children trace the numbers and say.

113

 Draw. 💬 Say.

How do we get from one place to another?

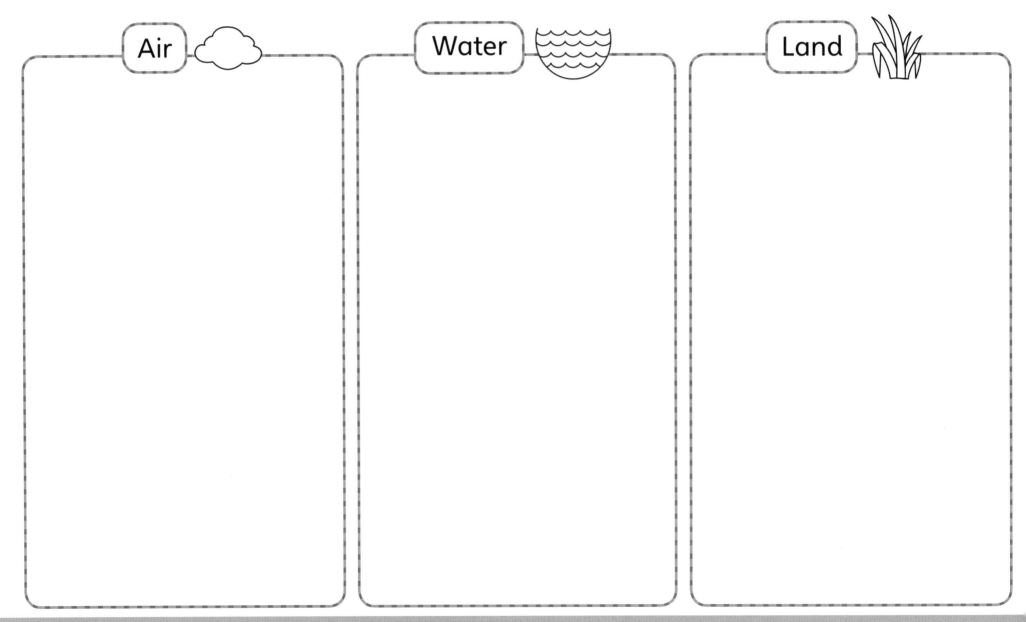

Air ☁	Water 〰	Land 🌱

Key Language: *car, train, bus, airplane, boat, bike, helicopter, ship, air, water, land, Where does a (bus) go? It goes in the air / water, on land. new, old, slow, fast, This (car) is (new), beach, amusement park, mountains, city, I'm going to the (beach). I'm going to get there (on a ship).* Ask the Big Question: *How do we get from one place to another?* Children look back through the unit to recall what they have learned. Then they draw an example of a type of transportation for each frame. Ask volunteers to share their drawings with the class and describe what they drew. Finally, answer the Big Question together, using the children's drawings to help.

9 What do plants need to grow?

🗨 Say. ✏ Color. ⬭ Trace.

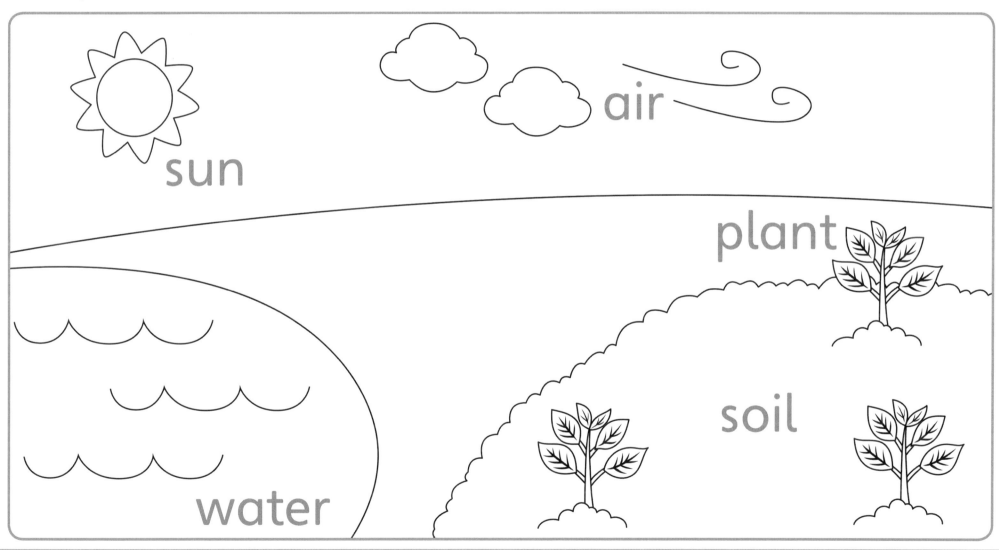

Key Language: *plant, sun, soil, water, air.* Children point and name the things in the picture. Then they color the elements and the plants. Optional: Children trace the words.

■ Say. ○ Circle. ✏ Color.

One Little Daffodil

Key Language: *What can you see? What's the story about? Who are the characters? What are they doing? Where does the story take place?, Ted, bell, plant.*
Children look at the story scenes. Ask the literacy questions. Then ask: *Can you see Ted? Can you see a bell? Can you see a plant?* Make sure children understand that Ted is the teacher and that flowers are plants. Children circle and then color the items in the pictures.

Say. ○ Circle. ✏ Color.

Key Language: *What can you see? What's the story about? Who are the characters? What are they doing? Where does the story take place?* Children look at the story scenes. Ask the literacy questions. Then ask: *Can you see three? Can you see happy faces?* Children circle and then color the items in the pictures. Then they retell the story in their own words. Provide language as needed.

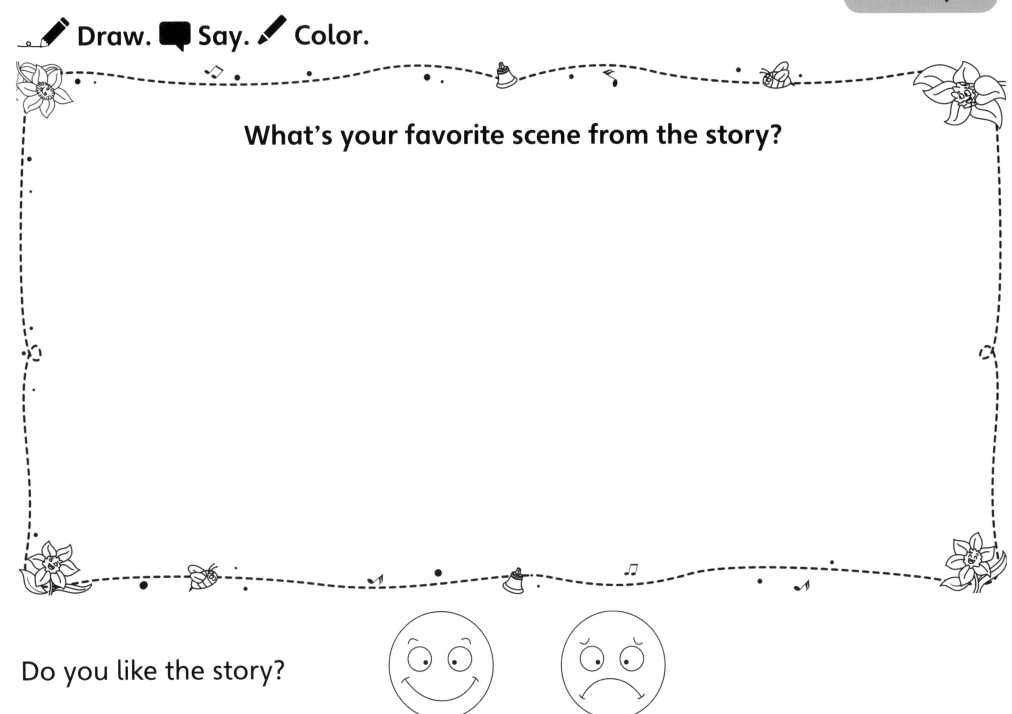

✏️ Draw. 💬 Say. 🖍 Color.

What's your favorite scene from the story?

Do you like the story?

Key Language: *What's your favorite scene?* Say: *Can you remember?* and discuss the story with the children. As you retell and talk about the story, stop and ask children: *Do you like the scene with the bee?* Children draw and color their favorite scene from the story. Then ask: *Do you like the story? (Yes. / No.)* Children color the happy face or the sad face.

 Look. 💬 Say. ✏️ Color.

Key Language: *Take care of plants.* Children look at the scene and describe it. Ask: *What is he doing? (Watering the plants.)* Then ask: *Is he taking care of the plants?* *(Yes!)* Discuss why it is important to take care of plants. *(So the plants are healthy and can help clean the air. So they can feed us. So they can make our environment beautiful.)* Finally, children color the boy taking care of the plants and the water helping the plants to grow.

119

 **Match.** **Say.** **Trace.**

seed   shovel   dig   hole   water   watering can

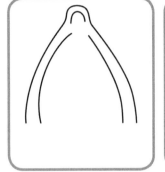  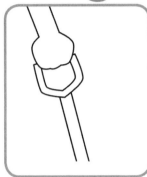 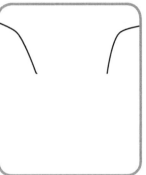  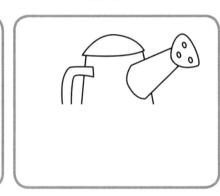

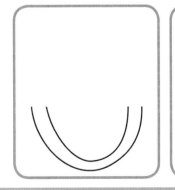   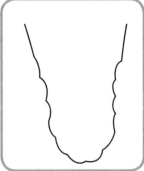 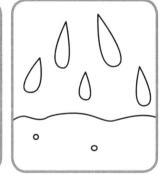 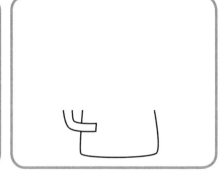

Key Language: *seed, shovel, hole, water, dig, watering can.* Children look at the pictures. Then they draw lines to match the halves of each item. Ask children to say the words as they finger trace between the halves, e.g., *seed-seed.* Optional: Children trace the words.

👁 Look. ◯ Trace. 🗨 Say.

1. First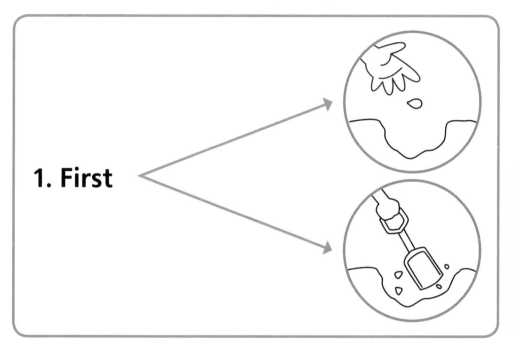

2. Then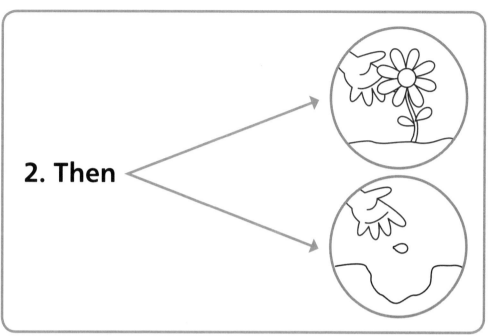

3. Next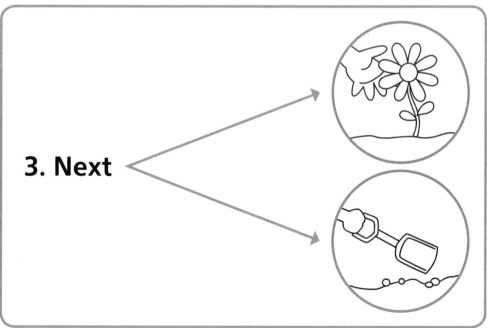

4. Finally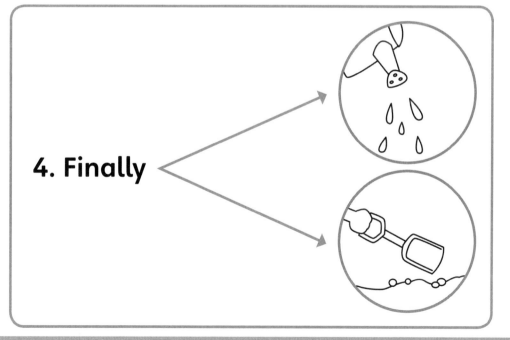

Key Language: *First, next, then, finally.* Look at the first frame together. Ask: *What happens first? Put the seed in the hole or dig the hole?* Discuss and guide children to the correct answer. (Dig the hole.) Children trace a circle around the correct picture. Continue with the remaining three steps: *put the seed in the hole. Cover the seed with soil. Water the seed.* Finally, children say the steps in order: *First, dig a hole with a shovel. Then, put the seed in the hole. Next, cover the seed with soil. Finally, water the seed with a watering can.*

👁 Look. 💬 Say. ✏️ Color.

Key Language: *tall, short, The (tree) is tall. S/he is short.* Children look at each group of pictures on the left of the page. Then they say the pattern: *short flower, tall flower, short flower.* Finally, children color the correct picture on the right to continue the sequence.

 Read. ✏️ Color. ⭕ Trace.

The **petals** are red.

The **leaves** are green.

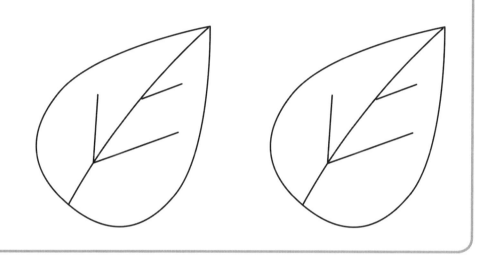

The **stem** is green.

The **roots** are brown.

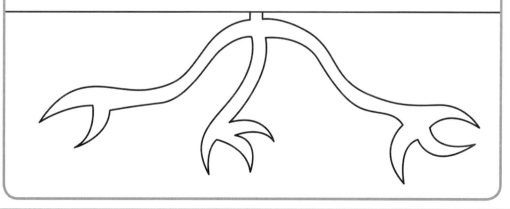

Key Language: *petals, stem, leaves, roots.* Read the first sentence together, with children following along. Children color the petals according to the sentence. Optional: They trace the word. Repeat with the remaining sentences and pictures.

👁 Look. ✏️ Draw. 💬 Say.

Key Language: *petals, leaves, roots, stem, What's missing? Which part is missing? The (petals / leaves / roots) are missing. The stem is missing.* Point to the first picture, the complete plant. Children name all the flower parts as you point to them: *petals, stem, leaves, roots.* Then they look at the second picture. Ask: *What's missing? Which part is missing?* Children draw the petals. Continue in this way with the other pictures. Finally, children point and say what each incomplete picture is missing, e.g., *The petals are missing.*

 **Draw.** 🗨 **Say.**

What are your favorite fruits?

Key Language: *What are your favorite fruits? My favorite fruits are ...* Point to the girl and read what she's saying: *What are your favorite fruits?* Invite volunteers to answer, and once you have lots of ideas, children draw their favorites on the page. Finally, children present their drawings, saying: *My favorite fruits are ...*

 Say. Trace. Color.

Key Language: *Where do (carrots) grow? (Carrots) grow underground. (Apples) grow on trees.* Children point to and name the fruits and vegetables on the page. Then they trace the fruits and vegetables and color them. Finally, ask volunteers to point to a fruit or vegetable and say where they grow: *Oranges grow on trees. Potatoes grow underground.*

 Count. ✏ Color. ⬭ Trace.

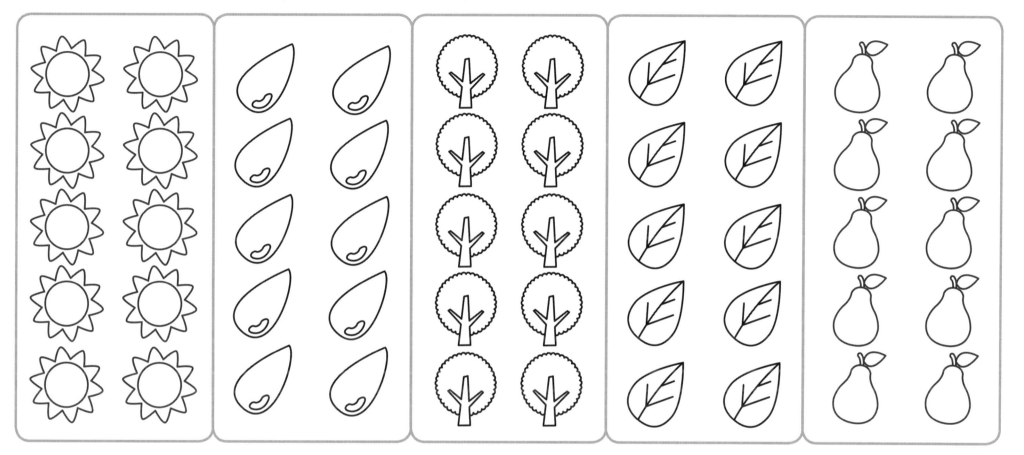

10 20 30 40 50

Key Language: *How many (leaves) can you see? Let's count by tens, Ten, twenty, thirty, forty, fifty, There are five sets of ten.* Point to the first frame and ask: *How many suns? Let's count.* Count to 10 together. Children color the 10 suns. Optional: Children trace the number 10 below. Continue with the second frame, asking: *How many seeds?* Count and color. Then say: *Let's count by tens: Ten, twenty!* Repeat with the remaining three frames, children coloring the 10 items each time and counting by tens together. Optional: Children trace the numbers and say.

127

 Draw. Say.

What do plants need to grow?

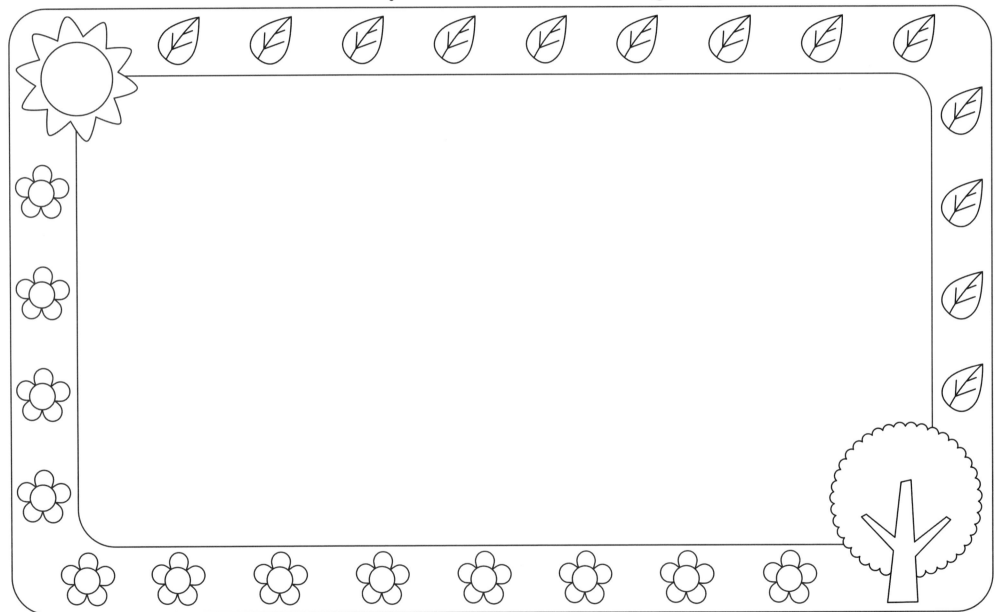

Key Language: *plant, sun, soil, water, air, seed, shovel, dig, hole, watering can, first, next, then, finally, petals, stem, leaves, roots, Which parts are missing? The (petals) are missing. Where do (fruits / vegetables) grow? They grow on trees / underground.* Ask the Big Question: *What do plants need to grow?* Children look back through the unit to recall what they have learned. Then they draw some of they things they have learned about inside the frame. Ask volunteers to share their drawings with the class and describe what they drew. Finally, answer the Big Question together, using the children's drawings to help.

Picture Dictionary

Children open the book to the corresponding unit. They point to a picture and name it. If children cannot name the vocabulary item, say the word and have them repeat it. Finally, children color the pictures.

129

Unit 1 / Vocabulary 1	Unit 1 / Vocabulary 2	Unit 1 / Vocabulary 3	Unit 2 / Vocabulary 1
paint	pencil	listen to stories	wash my face
draw	marker	sing songs	brush my hair
color	paintbrush	clean up	eat healthy food
cut	glue stick	eat lunch	put on a jacket
glue	scissors	play with friends	drink water

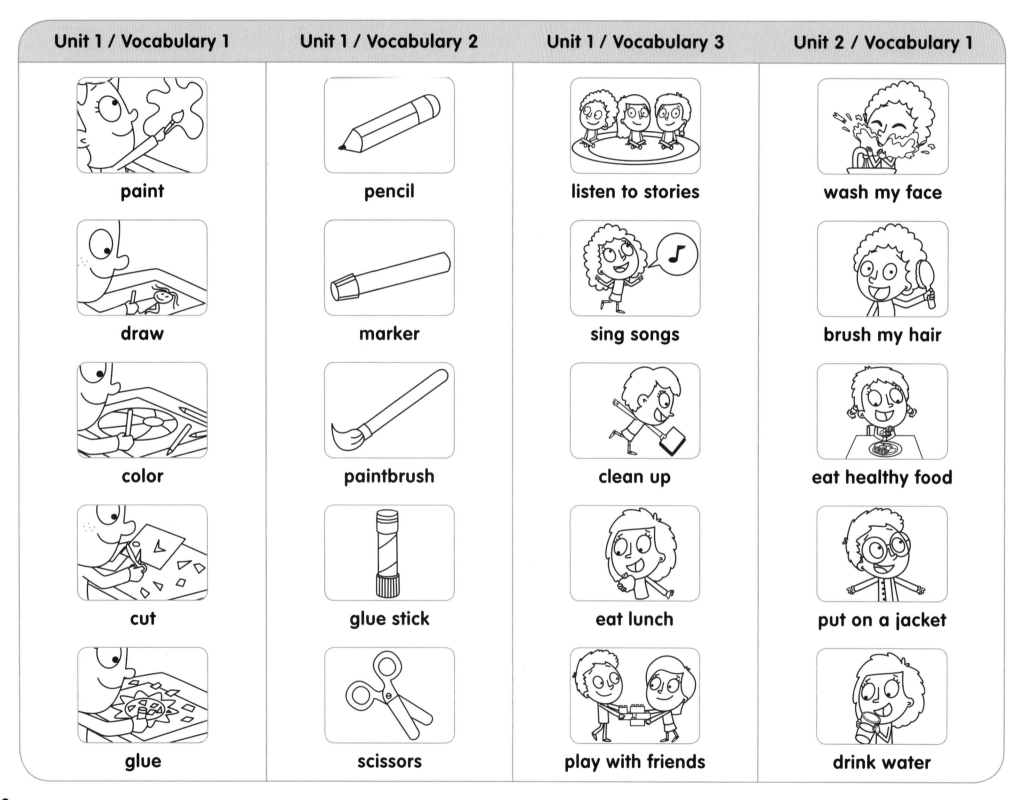

130

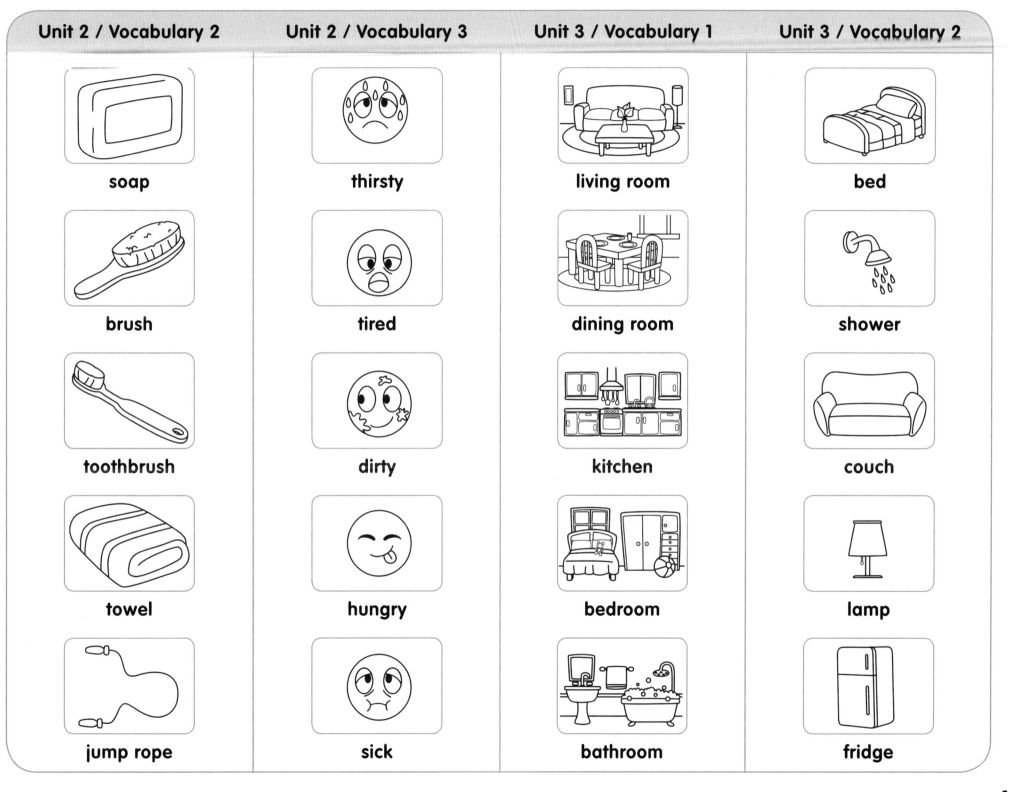

soap	thirsty	living room	bed
brush	tired	dining room	shower
toothbrush	dirty	kitchen	couch
towel	hungry	bedroom	lamp
jump rope	sick	bathroom	fridge

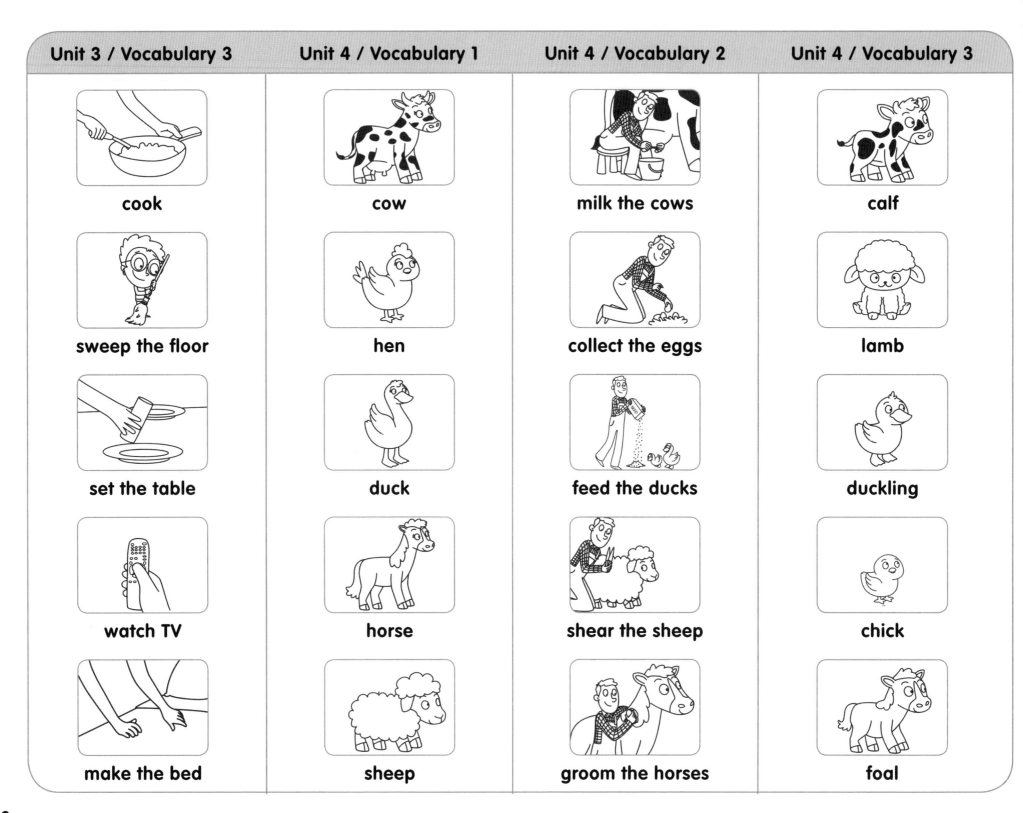

cook	cow	milk the cows	calf
sweep the floor	hen	collect the eggs	lamb
set the table	duck	feed the ducks	duckling
watch TV	horse	shear the sheep	chick
make the bed	sheep	groom the horses	foal

Unit 5 / Vocabulary 1	Unit 5 / Vocabulary 2	Unit 5 / Vocabulary 3	Unit 6 / Vocabulary 1
breakfast	water	milk	pants
lunch	pancakes	orange juice	shoes
dinner	soup	cereal	T-shirt
eggs	rice	fish	skirt
chicken		strawberries	sweater

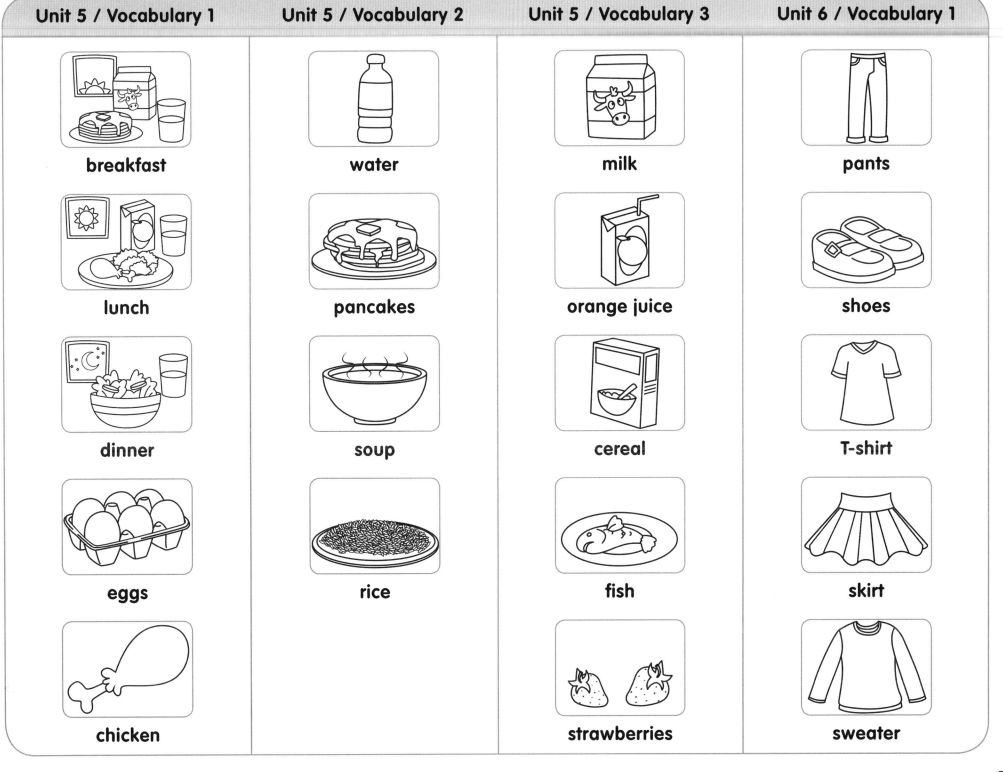

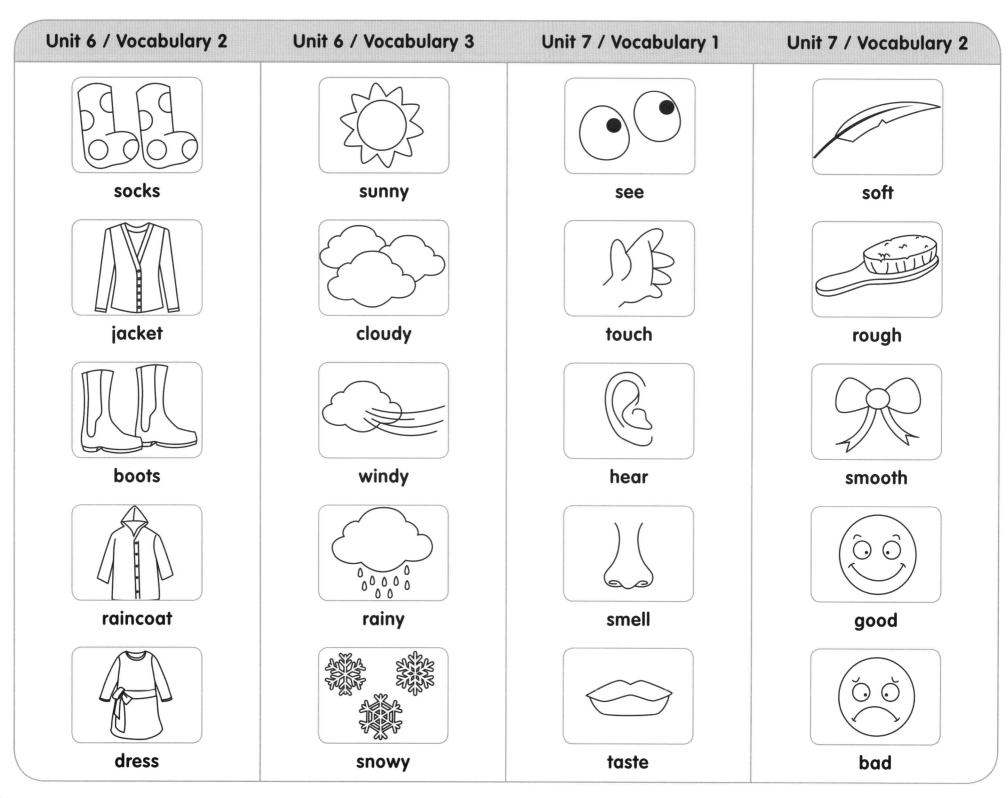

socks	sunny	see	soft
jacket	cloudy	touch	rough
boots	windy	hear	smooth
raincoat	rainy	smell	good
dress	snowy	taste	bad

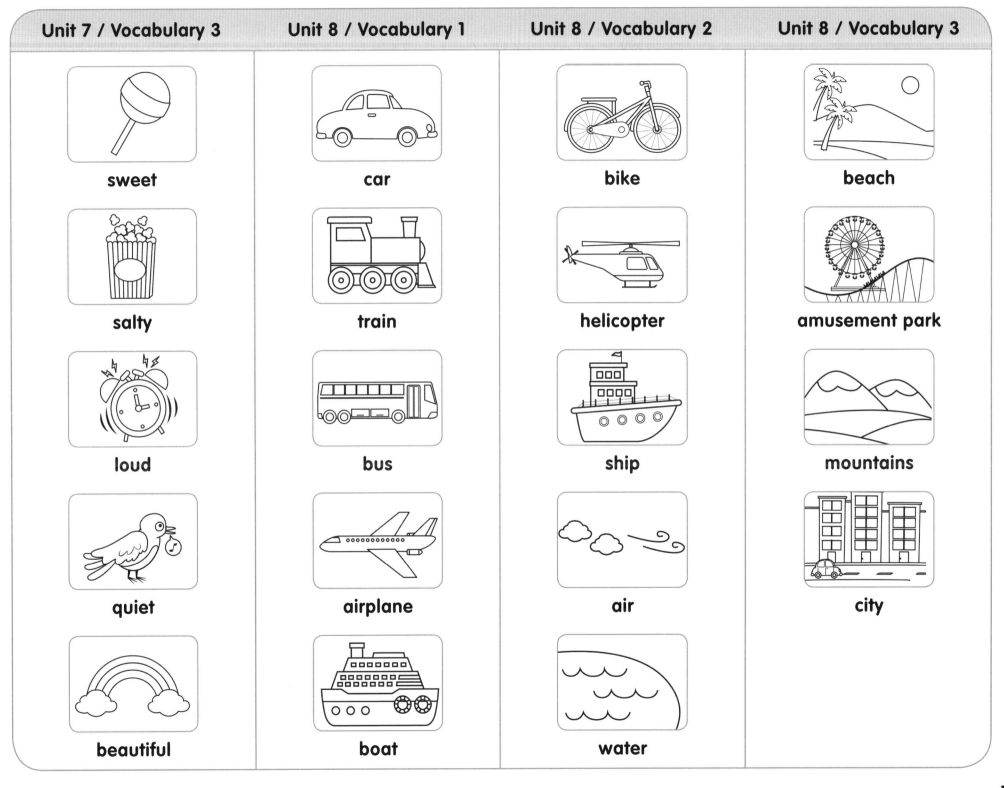

sweet	car	bike	beach
salty	train	helicopter	amusement park
loud	bus	ship	mountains
quiet	airplane	air	city
beautiful	boat	water	

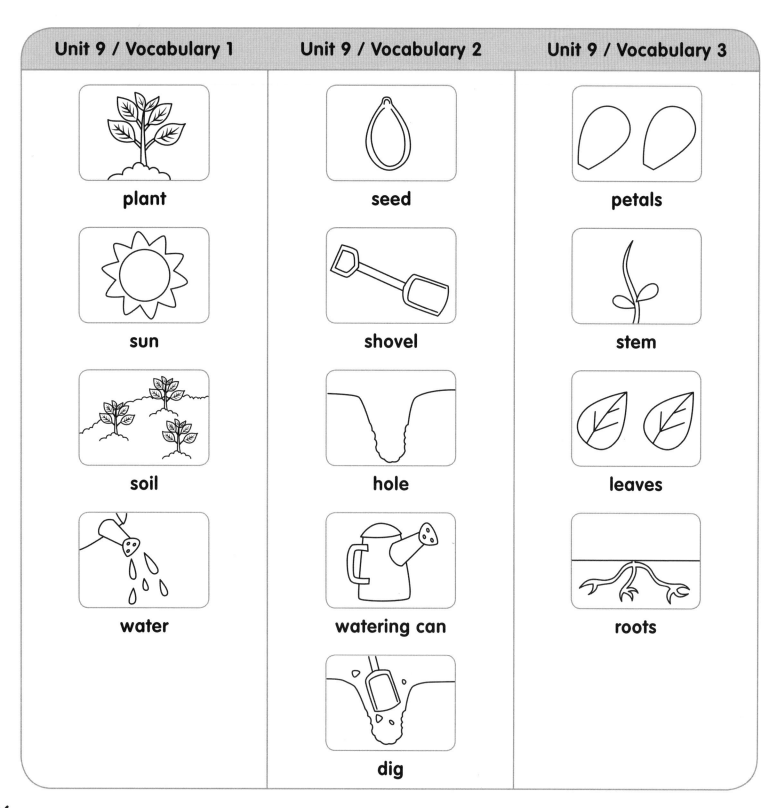

plant

sun

soil

water

seed

shovel

hole

watering can

dig

petals

stem

leaves

roots